It Happened In Arizona

Remarkable Events That Shaped History

Second Edition

James A. Crutchfield

Guilford, Connecticut

To the Memory of Wallace E. Clayton: writer, editor, friend

To buy books in quantity for corporate use
or incentives, call **(800) 962-0973**
or e-mail **premiums@GlobePequot.com**.

Previously published by Falcon Press Publishing Co., in 1994
The publisher gratefully acknowledges the assistance of Dr. James D. McBride, Department of History, Arizona State University.

Project editor: David Legere
Map: Daniel Lloyd © Morris Book Publishing, LLC

Library of Congress Cataloging-in-Publication Data is available on file.

ISBN 978-0-7627-5420-5

Printed in the United States of America

10 9 8 7 6 5 4 3 2 1

CONTENTS

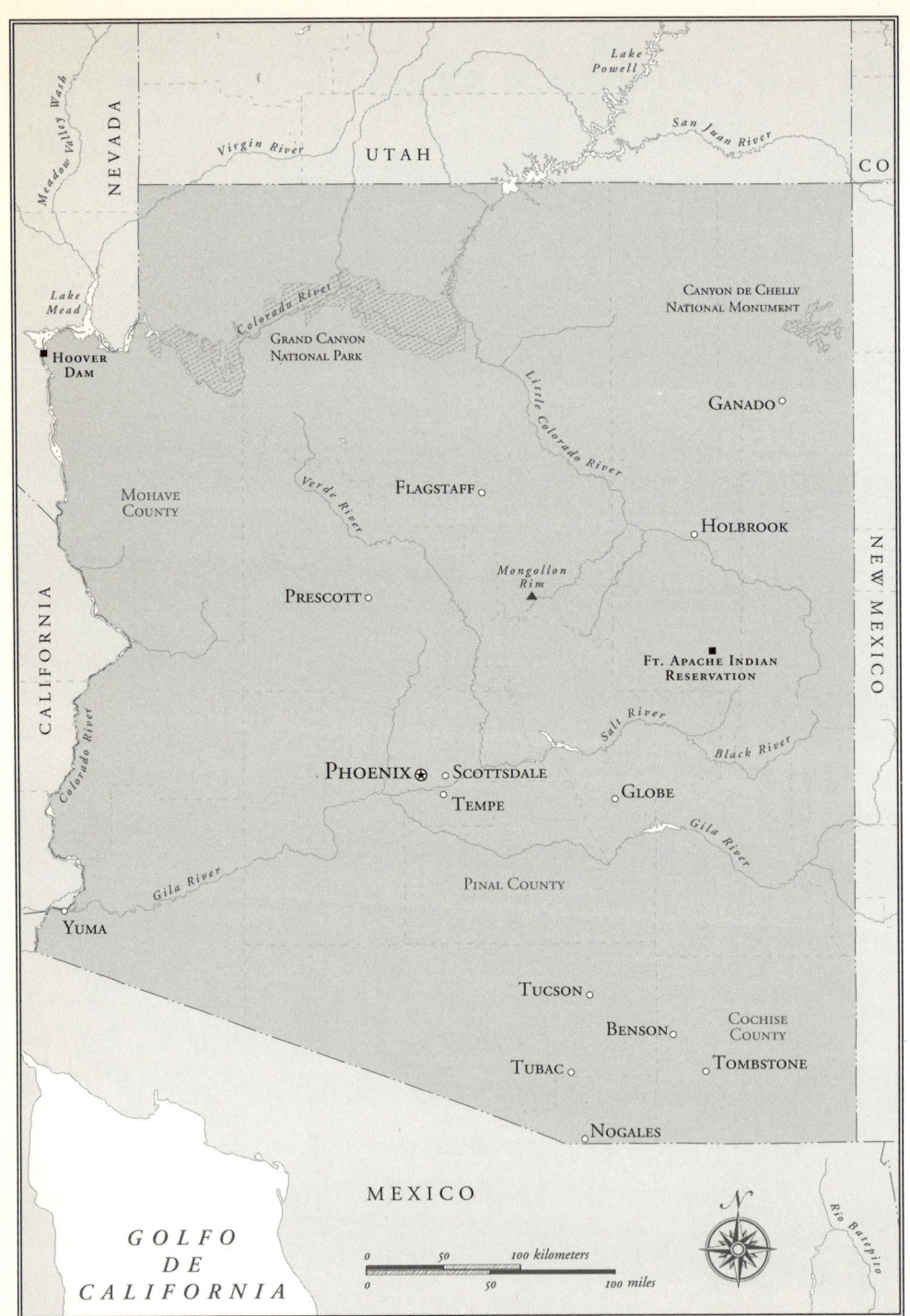

ARIZONA

CONTENTS

PREFACE

This book highlights some of the most fascinating episodes of Arizona history, from the days of the prehistoric Indians through modern times. Each story is complete in itself and can be read individually and out of sequence.

Arizona is an extremely important state historically, and although this book does not purport to be a thorough history of the Grand Canyon State, these vignettes have been chosen selectively to give the reader a broad and varied peek at Arizona's colorful past.

I hope that *It Happened in Arizona* will provide a few hours of pleasure to those who read it, and that it will, perhaps, find its way into the classrooms of the state, thereby giving younger generations a better appreciation of their vast heritage.

THE FIRST IRRIGATION EXPERIMENTS

A.D. 1200

It was clear to every member of the labor detail that they had done a good day's work. As the late summer sun hovered above the western horizon far across the desert, the men looked at one another and nodded their heads in approval. Then they prepared for the long trek back to the village several miles away.

Picking up their stone-tipped hoes and adzes, the workers headed east. They were weary. They had followed the same routine every day for several weeks—rising at dawn's first light, eating a sparse meal of dried beans and corn, picking up their primitive tools, and hiking from the village to the excavation site a few miles away. And the backbreaking work would continue for several months, since the irrigation canals the men were digging were far from complete.

Indeed, the leader of this particular work party estimated that several thousand more yards of canal, up to thirty feet wide and seven feet deep, had to be built this season. Then, when the new canals were linked with an existing system of ditches, new fields could be opened for the growing of beans, corn, squash, and cotton.

These canal diggers are known today as the Hohokam, and they occupied what is now south-central Arizona, near the confluence of the Salt and Gila Rivers. Historians are not certain of the Hohokam's origin. They may have been descendants of other Indian groups who had lived in the region since it was first populated about 11,000 years ago, or they may have migrated to the region from central Mexico. Whatever their origins, they appeared as a distinct culture about 300 B.C. and became the first people in the New World to cultivate crops through irrigation.

But by A.D. 1450, after centuries as one of the dominant cultures of the Southwest, they mysteriously vanished. It was the Pima Indians, who occupied the area later, who gave them their name. Hohokam is a Pima word meaning "all used up," or "those who have gone."

The Hohokam people were also the first in the New World to irrigate their crops. To plan miles of irrigation ditches and organize workforces of sufficient size and discipline to tackle such a monumental task, the Hohokam must not only have been socially organized, but technologically advanced as well.

An Australian archaeologist, V. Gordon Childe, in his book *What Happened in History,* alluded to the sophistication of a population that develops irrigation as a farming aid.

> *The digging and maintenance of irrigation channels are social tasks even more than the construction of defensive ramparts or the laying out of streets. The community as a whole must apportion to individual users the water thus canalized by collective effort.*

But it was not only in canal construction that the Hohokam people excelled. In later years, the culture was noted for its beautiful pottery and shell etchings, and expansive agricultural practices. Lieutenant Colonel William H. Emory, traveling with the Army of the West during the Mexican War, commented on the progressive farming techniques of the Pima Indians, whose culture succeeded that of the Hohokam. No doubt the description would hold basically true for the Pimas' predecessors as well.

> *We were at once impressed with the beauty, order, and disposition of the arrangements for irrigating and draining the land. Corn, wheat, and cotton are the crops of this peaceful and intelligent race of people. All the crops have been gathered in, and the stubbles show that they have been luxuriant. The cotton has been picked, and stacked for drying on the tops of sheds. The fields are sub-divided, by ridges of earth, into rectangles of about 200 X 100 feet for the convenience of irrigating.*

Captain A. R. Johnston, who accompanied Emory, was equally impressed with some of the ancient buildings left behind by the Hohokam people. Commenting on the complex that is today part of Casa Grande Ruins National Monument, Johnston wrote:

> *We saw to our left the "Casa de Montezuma." I rode to it, and found the remains of the walls of four buildings, and the piles of earth showing where many others had been. One of the buildings was still quite complete,*

as a ruin. The others had all crumbled but a few pieces of low, broken wall. The large casa *was 50 feet by 40, and had been four stories high, but the floors and roof had long since been burnt out. . . . There were four entrances—north, south, east, and west; the doors about four feet by two; the rooms as below and had the same arrangement on each story; there was no sign of a fireplace in the building. . . . The walls were four feet thick at the bottom, and had a curved inclination inwards to the top. . . . The walls had been smoothed outside, and plastered inside, and the surface still remained firm.*

The Hohokam culture was undoubtedly one of the most progressive in the Southwest. Along with their neighbors, the Ancestral Puebloan, Mogollon, Sinagua, and Salado, the Hohokam people transformed a vast, arid wasteland into a hospitable haven.

AN EARLY VIEW OF
THE GRAND CANYON

1540

It was late August 1540, and the noted Spanish captain-general, Francisco Vasquez de Coronado, with several of his lieutenants and some friendly Indian scouts, crouched over a map crudely drawn in the parched sand of the Southwestern desert. Coronado's eyes shifted from the Indians to his interpreter, who translated their incomprehensible words into pure, rhythmic Castilian Spanish.

Coronado and his command had arrived here in Cibola (near what is now the Arizona–New Mexico border) several days earlier, in search of the famous seven cities of gold that Fray Marcos had eagerly reported to exist in this region. Coronado had set forth from Compostela, Mexico, on February 23, along with 336 soldiers and about 700 Indians, herdsmen, wranglers, and other camp followers. Together they comprised "the most brilliant company ever assembled in the Indies to go in search of new lands," according to one chronicler of the time.

But, alas, Coronado and his men found no gold. Associates of Fray Marcos had described a town whose inhabitants "wear silk clothing down to their feet," a town which contained "a temple of their idols the walls of which . . . were covered with precious stones." Coronado found nothing but weathered adobe houses and hostile Zuni Indians wearing animal skins, cotton loincloths, and turkey-feather robes.

After two sorties in which several soldiers including Coronado were wounded, the conquistadors took the town of Hawikuh, scattering hundreds of terrified natives to neighboring villages. Rummaging through the defeated town, the soldiers found something they needed even more than gold. They found "corn, and beans, and fowl better than those of New Spain, and salt, the best and whitest I have seen in all my life," according to one eyewitness.

Now, after gorging themselves on the spoils of war, Coronado and his officers carefully studied the map traced in the sand. A scouting party had just returned from a reconnaissance of the region far to the west of Cibola. While visiting among the Hopi Indians, the scouts had heard rumors of a large river even farther west. Coronado decided to send an expedition to find this river.

A dozen horsemen led by Don Garcia Lopez de Cardenas left Cibola on August 25 and headed directly for the Hopi villages where news of the great river had originated. At the town of Tusayan, Cardenas asked for several Hopi guides to lead the party to its destination.

For several days, Cardenas and his followers traveled across the desert of what is now northern Arizona. Suddenly, they came upon the Grand Canyon of the Colorado River at some unknown point on its southern rim. One can only imagine the awestruck expressions on the faces of the conquistadors as they viewed the magnificent layers of multicolored rock that stretched endlessly in both directions. At the bottom of the mile-deep canyon was the very river they were looking for: the winding Colorado.

Although he did not accompany the expedition to the Grand Canyon, Pedro de Castaneda, a contemporary chronicler, did record eyewitness testimony of some of the men who did.

This country was elevated and full of low twisted pines, very cold, and lying open toward the north, so that, although this was the warm season, no one could live there on account of the cold. They passed three days along this canyon looking for a passage down to the river, which looked from above as if the water was a fathom's width across, although the Indians said it was half a league wide. To descend was impossible, for after these three days, Captain Melgosa and one Juan Galeras and another companion, who were the most agile men, made an attempt to go down at the least difficult place, and descended until those who were above were unable to keep sight of them because of the rock overhang. They returned about four o'clock in the afternoon, not having succeeded in reaching the bottom on account of the great difficulties which they found, because what seemed to be easy from above was not so, but instead very rough and steep. They said that they had been down about a third of the way and that the river seemed very large from the place which they reached, and that from what they saw they thought the Indians had given the width correctly. From the rim, some small pinnacles on the sides of the cliffs seemed to be about as tall as a man, but those

who went down swore that when they reached these
rocks they were bigger than the great tower at Seville.

Today, millions of visitors view the Grand Canyon annually, standing in awe much as those first Spanish soldiers did more than 450 years ago. When President Theodore Roosevelt viewed the canyon in 1903, he remarked, "You cannot improve on it. The ages have been at work on it, and man can only mar it." In 1908, he ensured that the Grand Canyon would be preserved for posterity by declaring it a national monument. In 1919, it became a national park.

In the 1960s, the Grand Canyon was jeopardized by a proposed reclamation project that called for the construction of two high dams along the course of the Colorado River. Fortunately, after a strong and spirited national outcry, the plan was dropped, and today a visitor can enjoy the same wild and savage beauty of the mighty Colorado that impressed a dozen Spanish conquistadors in 1540.

THE ARRIVAL OF FATHER KINO

1687

The weather was cool on that day in early 1687 when Eusebio Francisco Kino, a missionary with the Society of Jesus, reached his destination in today's Mexican state of Sonora. The good father had left Mexico City on November 20, 1686, and had finally arrived on the frontier of New Spain, ready to share Christianity with the native people of this remote desert region.

Father Kino had come a long way from his humble beginnings. Once described as "the incomparable pioneer of the Southwest and Pacific Coast," he was not Spanish as were many of his associates. Rather, he was born in northern Italy in 1645. He received a good education for the times, excelled in mathematics, but later forsook a teaching position at a university for missionary work as a Jesuit.

Father Kino traveled to Mexico in 1681, along with several other young Jesuits whose mission it was to save the souls of "pagan" Indians. Lower California beckoned to Kino first, and in 1683 he sailed there from Mexico, ready to begin his New World proselytizing. A little more than two years later, the mission work in Lower California was suspended.

Kino returned to Mexico City, where he was eventually given the job of converting Pimeria Alta, a vast region of New Spain that encompassed much of what is now the northern part of Sonora and the southern part of Arizona. It was here, in the land of the Pima Indians, that Kino would make his most indelible mark on the history of the Southwest.

When Father Kino arrived in Sonora in 1687, he immediately set to work building a mission which he named Nuestra Senora de los Dolores (Our Lady of Sorrows). From there, the priest and his helpers would minister to this vast desert domain.

Over the next several years, Kino made thirteen trips into Arizona and established many additional missions there and in Sonora. The most notable in Arizona were San Xavier del Bac, Tumacacori, and Guevavi. The remains of all three can still be seen along Interstate 19, south of Tucson. San Xavier is still used by worshippers today.

Among the Indians to whom Father Kino ministered were the Pimas and the Tohono O'odham (formerly known as the Papagos). Both were agricultural tribes that eked out a living from the desert soil. Kino favored the Pimas, descendants of the prehistoric Hohokam people of the same region. Herbert E. Bolton, in his biography of Kino, *The Padre on Horseback,* noted that,

> *to the Pimas, Kino was the Great White Father. They loved him, he loved them, and they were ready to die for each other. To him they flocked as if drawn by a magnet. From northeast, north, northwest, and west they beat trails to the door of the missionary wizard. Chiefs and warriors went to attend councils; to take part in church fiestas; to be baptized; to assist in*

planting, harvesting, and roundups. They had a child-ish desire to satisfy Kino's every wish.

The Pimas' love and respect were returned in kind. These Indians often were blamed for strife and bloodshed caused by the far-roaming Apaches. According to Bolton, Kino religiously stood by his friends and defended them against these false accusations with "the full force of his ever ready pen."

During almost a quarter of a century in Pimeria Alta, Father Kino saved more than 48,000 souls, built 29 missions, and traveled thousands of miles from one end of his domain to the other. In addition to being the spiritual leader of thousands of converted Indians, he was a rancher of some note. He established cattle herds at several of his missions, not only to feed the Indians but also to make the churches less financially dependent upon government subsidies.

Father Kino died at Magdalena, Mexico, in 1711, at the age of sixty-six. Father Agustin de Campos, who had been Kino's faithful companion for the previous eighteen years, wrote of the passing of this man who left such a legacy to Arizona.

Father Kino died in the year 1711, having spent twenty-four years in glorious labors in this Pimeria. . . . He died as he had lived, with extreme humility and poverty. . . . He died in the house of the Father where he had gone to dedicate a finely made chapel in his pueblo of Santa Magdalena. . . . When he was singing the Mass of the dedication he felt indisposed, and it seems that the Holy Apostle . . . was calling him, in order that . . . he might accompany him . . . in glory.

A BATTLE WITH
THE TOHONO O'ODHAM

1827

In late January 1826, according to his own testimony (or more likely 1827 since some of his dates have been found to be inaccurate), James Ohio Pattie and a small group of trappers approached a Tohono O'odham Indian village near the forks of the Salt and Gila Rivers, just west of today's city of Phoenix. The Indians did not seem very friendly as they "came running to meet us, with their faces painted, and their bows and arrows in their hands," Pattie later wrote.

Originally from Kentucky but lately from Missouri, Pattie hesitated to mingle with the Tohono O'odham for fear of treachery. However, the other members of his expedition, mostly French-Americans under the command of Miguel Robidoux, milled about the village and exchanged pleasantries with its inhabitants.

Pattie warned Robidoux that the Indians were up to no good, but the leader refused to listen to him, and at one point he even accused Pattie of cowardice. Nevertheless, Pattie and another uneasy trapper pitched their camp a good distance from the Indian village.

They made sure they were packed and ready to retreat to the mountains if the Indians attacked. The rest of the trappers bedded down for the night among the Tohono O'odham.

"Around midnight," according to Pattie's narrative,

> we heard a fierce whistle, which we instantly understood to be the signal for an attack on the French camp. But a moment ensued, before we heard the clashing of war clubs, followed by shrieks and heavy groans of the dying French, mingled with the louder and more horrible yells of these treacherous and blood thirsty savages. A moment afterwards, we heard a party of them making towards us. To convince them that they could not butcher us in our defenceless sleep, we fired upon them. This caused them to retreat. Convinced that we had no time to lose, we mounted our horses, and fled at the extent of our speed. . . . We took our direction toward a high mountain on the south side of the river, and . . . reached the mountain at day break.

From their perch on the mountain, Pattie and his companion saw far in the distance a figure coming toward them. As the man drew nearer, they saw that it was a badly wounded Robidoux. As Pattie ministered to the Frenchman's wounds, Robidoux told his story. All of the trappers had foolishly stacked their arms for the night, but Robidoux had kept a pistol hidden in his clothing. When the Tohono O'odham attacked, he fired and gained enough time to escape, but not before being wounded several times. According to Pattie, the French captain apologized for his insulting manner of the night before. "He observed in a tone apparently of deep compunction, that if he had had the good sense and good temper to have listened to my apprehensions and cautions, both he and his people might have been now gaily riding over the prairies," Pattie later wrote.

The three wanderers finally met another trapping party led by an American, Ewing Young. The men immediately made plans for revenge. Marching back to the Indian village, the group of thirty-two lured the Tohono O'odham into an ambush by posing two men in clear view of the warriors. Pattie described the scene.

> *They raised the yell, and ran towards the two persons, who instantly dropped down under the bank. There must have been at least 200 in pursuit. They were in a moment close on the bank. In order to prevent the escape of the two men, they spread into a kind of circle to surround them. This brought the whole body abreast of us. We allowed them to approach within twenty yards, when we gave them our fire. They commenced a precipitate retreat, we loading and firing as fast as was in our power. . . . In less than ten minutes, the village was so completely evacuated, that not a human being was to be found, save one poor old blind and deaf Indian who sat eating his mush as unconcernedly as if all had been tranquil in the village. We did not molest him.*

Pattie reported in his narrative that his party killed 110 Indians that day. They burned the Tohono O'odham village, and buried the French trappers' bodies.

Pattie eventually gave up his trapper's life and gravitated back to Kentucky, where he enrolled at Augusta College. His book, *The Personal Narrative of James O. Pattie, of Kentucky,* was published in 1831 in Cincinnati. No one knows what became of Pattie in later years. He probably died in the cholera epidemic that hit Kentucky in 1833. Whatever his fate, he is remembered today as one of the first white Americans to frequent the Arizona wilderness.

COLONEL COOKE'S MARCH THROUGH TUCSON

1846

Lieutenant Colonel Philip St. George Cooke must have wondered why he and and his battalion had met no serious resistance from Mexicans as they traveled from Sante Fe to Tucson in December 1846. After all, the United States was at war with Mexico. Even though General Stephen Watts Kearny had occupied Santa Fe the previous August without shedding a drop of blood, one still would have expected a skirmish now and then.

After taking Santa Fe, Kearny had appointed a civilian governor, the well-known and respected trader Charles Bent, to manage affairs in New Mexico. Then the general had split his Army of the West into four elements. One of them, Cooke's command, was charged with blazing a wagon road from Santa Fe to the Pacific. With Cooke were about 450 Mormon volunteers with no military training and very little discipline.

As Cooke's troops approached Tucson, the colonel decided to march directly through town. Although there was a route around the village and although Tucson housed a garrison of Mexican soldiers armed with artillery, Cooke's men needed supplies. Besides, the route through town was reported to be better and shorter than the one around it.

As Cooke neared the garrison, he met a company of Mexican dragoons. Their sergeant relayed a request from the fort's commander that the Americans bypass Tucson. Later that night, two Mexican couriers rode into Cooke's camp with orders that he was to go around the village and have no communication with its residents.

Cooke rejected these terms and demanded instead that the garrison at Tucson refrain from raising arms against the United States for the duration of the war. He also insisted that his men have the freedom to trade with the townspeople. The couriers left at once, assuring Cooke that their commander would never agree to such a treaty.

According to Cooke's official report of his journey to California, the unexpected then happened.

> *About five miles from town I was met by a dragoon, or lancer, who delivered me a letter, simply refusing my terms. I told him there was no answer, and he rode off. I then ordered all arms to be loaded. Immediately afterward, two citizens rode up, and reported that the place had been evacuated. I arrived at 1 o'clock, and, having passed through the fort, encamped in the edge of town. Two small field pieces had been taken off, and all public property of value, except for a large store of wheat.*

Tucson, the northernmost *presidio* built by the Spanish in today's state of Arizona, was completed in the late 1700s as a defense against the Apache Indians. When Cooke arrived in 1846, the village had fallen into disrepair, but it still boasted the fort, with walls 750 feet long and almost 12 feet high. A few hundred impoverished Mexicans called Tucson home, and after Cooke assured them that he and his men were not enemies, they became friendly and brought the Americans food.

During his stay in Tucson, Cooke wrote a letter to the governor of Sonora, the Mexican province in which the town was located. Cooke had concluded that Sonorans were unhappy with the Mexican government because it failed to provide proper protection from the Apaches. Written to capitalize on these hard feelings, the letter read, in part:

> *The undersigned, marching in command of a battalion of United States infantry, from New Mexico to California, has found it convenient for the passage of his wagon train, to cross the frontier of Sonora. . . . I have found it necessary to take this presidio [Tucson] in route to the Gila. Be assured that I did not come as an enemy of the people whom you govern; they have received only kindness at my hands. . . . Sonora refused to contribute to the support of the present war against my country, alleging the excellent reasons that all her resources were necessary to her defence from the incessant attacks of savages; that the central government gave her no protection, and was therefore entitled to no support. . . . Thus one part of Mexico allies itself against another. The unity of Sonora with the [United] States of the north, now her neighbors, is necessary effectually to subdue these . . . Apaches.*

Cooke and his Mormon Battalion left Tucson after two days and continued their mission to open a wagon road through the Arizona wilderness. They arrived at San Diego on January 29, 1847, after marching 1,125 miles in 102 days. Without knowing it at the time, Cooke was making history, and in a few short years his wagon trail would become the basis for the popular and much-traveled Gila Road across southern Arizona.

THE MAKING OF A GHOST TOWN

1849

Many of the ghost towns that haunt the American West owe their existence to the boom-bust nature of mining. But the ghost town that Benjamin Butler Harris entered on July 7, 1849, was not a victim of the economy. The village of Tubac, located just north of the present border between Arizona and Mexico, had met its death at the hands of the relentless Apaches.

Harris visited Tubac on his way to the West Coast. Originally a schoolteacher from Tennessee, he had been practicing law in Panola County, Texas, when he learned of the California gold strike. He was weary of the humid East Texas climate. Complaining that, "for about eight months of each year, malarious fever like a juggling devil assaulted me front and rear and hung like an incubus upon my constitution," he packed his belongings and joined a caravan to California.

The route from Texas to California left the United States at El Paso and traversed the northern reaches of the Mexican states of Chihuahua and Sonora. It reentered the nation at Yuma, on the

Colorado River. Much of the trail followed a wagon road laid out by Lieutenant Colonel Philip St. George Cooke just three years earlier. The United States would buy the region between Texas and California and south of the Gila River from Mexico in 1853.

Harris left his impressions of Tubac and the surrounding countryside in a journal he kept during his journey.

> *Passing a few miles up the Santa Cruz Valley and turning to the left through a low pass in the mountains, we came to the deserted town of Tubac. From the number of houses and the manner in which Mexicans occupy them, I judged that its population must have been recent, for the wheat crop in the fields was ripe for the sickle. The bell and costly pictures, with other ornaments, were still in the church. Peaches and other fruits were ripening on the trees. Streets were uninvaded by weeds and the buildings still shone with new whitewash. There was not a human soul to enliven this silence. It was a most eloquent stillness.*

Tubac was indeed a ghost town. Its narrow streets and battered buildings seemed to scream with despair. Harris continued:

> *When our men rang the church bell, its hollow echoes seemed a bellowing mockery of all things human. Our voices seemed unnatural and ghostly. It was a gloomy solitude—far more so than the loneliest desert. Every house was pepper-boxed with portholes. Ancient bullet marks on walls showed a very warm and desperate*

conflict. . . . About six months before, the entire people
and city became a clotted mass of blood at the hands of
hundreds of . . . Indian besiegers.

Tubac had been founded in 1752 as a Spanish *presidio,* the first
in present-day Arizona. Originally, it had been called San Ignacio
de Tubac, and its purpose was to protect the local inhabitants from
continuous Apache raids. The garrison was manned by about fifty
soldiers, but it proved ineffective. Over the years, the village was
abandoned again and again as the hostile Apaches brazenly attacked
the civilized outposts of the Spanish and later the Mexicans.

By July 1852, Tubac was populated again, although the town
was in decay. John Russell Bartlett, the American representative on
the Mexican Boundary Commission, visited the village then and was
not impressed.

In a book of travels in a strange country, one is
expected to describe every town he visits; but as for this
God-forsaken place, when I have said that it contains
a few dilapidated buildings, and an old church, with
a miserable population, I have said about all. It was
established as a presidio almost a century and a half
ago, and usually maintained a population of four hun-
dred souls. It was abandoned a year before our arrival,
but had since been repopulated, and might have com-
prised at the time of our visit a hundred souls.

After Harris left Tubac, he continued to California, where he
prospected for several months before becoming disenchanted and
returning to the practice of law.

THE ORDEAL OF THE OATMAN GIRLS

1851

Royce Oatman must have been a bit uneasy on this March day in 1851. After all, he, his wife Mary Ann, and their seven children had left their farm in northern Illinois far behind them. After months of torturous travel, they had reached the hostile Indian territory of the Southwest, spurred on by the dream of building a utopian community on the banks of the Colorado River.

The Oatmans had left Independence, Missouri, in the summer of 1850, as part of a train of twenty wagons, fifty people, and a herd of cattle. At the direction of the Mormon leader James Brewster, the party planned to establish a "New Zion" near what is now the border between California and Arizona.

The Oatmans eventually left the wagon train along with two other families, the Wilders and the Kellys. For almost a month, they all lingered at a friendly Pima Indian village on the Gila River, northwest of Tucson. Now, Oatman was anxious to move on—so anxious that he chose to begin the last leg of this difficult journey without the Wilders and the Kellys. He was apprehensive about this decision to go it alone.

On March 19, as the Oatman wagons creaked along the Gila River about eighty miles east of its confluence with the Colorado, they met a small party of Yavapai Indians who asked for tobacco and bread. Although the Oatmans had little to spare, Royce complied. But the Indians demanded even more food. Afraid he would not be able to feed his family, Oatman refused.

Instantly, the Yavapai attacked the wagon train and killed everyone except fifteen-year-old Lorenzo, who was left for dead; his fourteen-year-old sister Olive; and a younger sister, Mary Ann. The two terrified girls were taken captive.

At the Yavapai village, the girls were treated roughly by the Indian women and put to work as slaves. Lorenzo was rescued by passing emigrants and taken to Fort Yuma, California, where he recovered from his wounds. Eventually, he gravitated to San Francisco. He worked ceaselessly to free his sisters from the Indians.

Sometime in early 1852, the Yavapai sold Olive and Mary Ann to a party of Mojave Indians, who lived about 150 miles up the Colorado River from Fort Yuma. The Mojaves treated the frightened girls with more kindness than the Yavapai. Olive later recalled:

> We were conducted immediately to the home of the chief,
> and welcomed with the staring eyes of collecting groups
> and an occasional smile from the members of the chief's
> family, who gave the warmest expressions of joy. . . . The
> chief's house was a beautiful but small elevation crown-
> ing the river bank, from which the eye could sweep a
> large section of the valley and survey the entire village, a
> portion of which lined each bank of the stream.

Even though life was easier with the Mojaves, Olive and Mary Ann still dreamed of being free again. After months of captivity, Mary

Ann died of malnutrition. Olive was fully adopted into the tribe, even having her face tattooed in the traditional manner of Mojave women.

In 1855, Henry Grinnell, a civilian employee at Fort Yuma, learned that the Mojaves had a white woman living in their village. He approached Lieutenant Colonel Martin Burke, the commandant of the fort, with a plan to rescue Olive. Grinnell suggested that a Yuma Indian named Francisco, who was friendly with the Mojaves, should go to their village and attempt to ransom the girl. On January 27, 1856, Burke wrote the following letter, which Francisco carried on his mission.

> *Francisco, Yuma Indian, bearer of this, goes to the*
> *Mohave Nation to obtain a white woman there,*
> *named Olivia* [sic]. *It is desirable that she should come*
> *to this post, or send her reasons why she does not wish*
> *to come.*

Francisco succeeded in bringing Olive to Fort Yuma. After five years among the Indians, the young woman had almost forgotten English, but in time she recovered both mentally and physically from her ordeal. Lorenzo, now living in Los Angeles, immediately headed for Fort Yuma and a long-awaited reunion with his sister.

Olive became an overnight celebrity. With Lorenzo, she toured California and met Royal B. Stratton, a minister who volunteered to act as her publicist. In 1857, Stratton published a book, *Life among the Indians: Being an Interesting Narrative of the Captivity of the Oatman Girls.* The book became an instant best seller and was reissued several times over the next few years under the title *Captivity of the Oatman Girls.*

Stratton's book is part of a distinct genre of American historical literature called "Indian Captivities." There are hundreds of such narratives depicting the plights of unfortunate whites taken prisoner by various Indian tribes, from the earliest settlement of America to the late nineteenth century. James Levernier and Hennig Cohen, two modern compilers, in their book *The Indians and their Captives*, make the following interesting point:

> *After the Revolutionary War, when Indians became the main obstacle to frontier expansion, the captivity narratives became almost exclusively a device for anti-Indian propaganda. A few narratives presented a sympathetic picture of Indian life, but most were shaped by publishers exploiting a mass market that thrived on sensationalism, in a natural alliance with land speculators who wanted to implement a policy of Indian extermination in the interest of real estate development. Accounts like . . . R. B. Stratton's* Captivity of the Oatman Girls . . . *among dozens of others, were designed to horrify audiences into hating what the novelist Hugh Henry Brackenridge . . . an editor of captive narratives, referred to as "the animals, vulgarly called Indians. . . ." In them, the Indian is painted so irredeemably brutish that he deserves to be deprived of his lands.*

Olive eventually married John B. Fairchild in New York, lived in Michigan for a few years, and finally moved with her husband and children to Sherman, Texas. She died in 1903. Lorenzo died in Nebraska in 1901.

AN EXCURSION INTO
NORTHERN ARIZONA

1851

Captain Lorenzo Sitgreaves of the U.S. Corps of Topographical Engineers had no doubt read of Coronado's journeys through northern Arizona in 1540. And he was most likely familiar with the saga of Coronado's lieutenant, Cardenas, who was the first known white man to lay eyes on the Grand Canyon of the Colorado River. Sitgreaves must have been intrigued by Cardenas's vivid description of the great chasm. But now, on this warm November day in 1851, only a few days journey from the canyon himself, he had to make the difficult decision to bypass it.

Sitgreaves had been charged with tracing the course of the Zuni River from its headwaters to its junction with the Colorado, "determining its course and character." He was then to "pursue the Colorado to its junction with the Gulf of Mexico." It was not until he had followed the entire course of the Zuni—noting that it was "not entitled to the name of river; in most parts of our country it would not be dignified with that of creek"—that he discovered that the stream flowed not into the Colorado, but into the Little Colorado River.

Sitgreaves was in the San Francisco Mountains near today's city of Flagstaff when he decided not to follow the Little Colorado to its junction with the Colorado near the Grand Canyon. In his official account of his journey, presented to the U.S. Senate in 1853, he explained this decision.

> *I had designed to explore the river [the Little Colorado] upward to the great canon . . . but the exhausted condition of the animals and scanty supply of provisions (the party having been already several days on reduced rations) compelled me reluctantly to forego my purpose.*

Instead, Sitgreaves and his small engineering party turned westward and headed cross-country for a spot on the Colorado River far below the Grand Canyon. Sitgreaves was unimpressed with the two hundred or so miles of Arizona landscape that lay between the San Francisco Mountains and the Colorado. In his report, he devoted only a single paragraph to describing the region he crossed.

> *The whole country traversed from the San Francisco mountains was barren and devoid of interest. It consists of mountain ranges and desert plains, the latter having an average height of about 5,000 feet above the level of the ocean. The larger growth, almost exclusively of cedar, was confined to the mountains; and the scanty vegetation of the plains, parched by a long drought, furnished few specimens for the botanist.*

Fortunately, Sitgreaves was more explicit in some of his other descriptions. For example, he provided one of the earliest accounts of the Mojave Indians, who lived along the lower Colorado River. This sizable tribe was an exception to the general rule that most farming cultures are peaceful. Fearless warriors, the Mojaves had already gained a nasty reputation among whites. In an 1827 affair known as the Mojave Massacre, they had harassed mountain man Jedediah Smith and his followers as the party tried to reach California. Now, a quarter of a century later, the tribe was approachable but still belligerent.

Sitgreaves described the Mojaves in his Senate report.

The appearance of the Mohave is striking . . . the men averaging at least six feet in height; and their stalwart and athletic figures offered a convincing proof of the excellence of a vegetable diet. Almost all the men were naked, with the exception of the breech-cloth. The hair, cut square across the brows in front, hung in loose braids behind, reaching frequently as low as the waist. . . . The only garment worn by the women was a long fringe of strips of willow-bark wound around the waist, and falling as low as the knees. No covering to the feet was worn by either sex. Their arms are the bow and arrow, the spear and the club. The arrow is formed of two pieces—that to which the barb is attached, of hard wood, seven inches long, or one-fourth the entire length; and the other of a light reed that grows profusely along the banks of the river, feathered, as usual, at the extremity. . . . Their lodges are rectangular, formed of upright posts imbedded in the ground, and rudely thatched on the top and three sides.

Sitgreaves was among the first white men to explore that expanse of northern Arizona that stretches from the present-day New Mexican border to California. By documenting his journey, he brought to the attention of the American public an area that few had even been aware existed.

THE GREAT RAILROAD SURVEY

1853

In early 1853, national attention was focused on the region that in a decade would become the Arizona Territory. One of the most pressing problems facing the westward-looking American government at the time was where to route a transcontinental railroad. The issue had torn the nation apart. In the halls of Congress, politicians and lobbyists from the North and South fought to have the rail line routed through their own regions.

At the center of the controversy were two well-known men: Jefferson Davis, the U.S. secretary of war, and Thomas Hart Benton, a former senator from Missouri. Several alternate routes from the Mississippi River to the Pacific Ocean had already been proposed. Naturally Davis, a Southerner, preferred one that traversed the southern sections of the country. Benton scoffed at the idea of running a railroad through the arid Southwest. The terrain, he argued, was "so utterly desolate, desert, and God-forsaken that Kit Carson says a wolf could not make a living on it." Benton's preference, not surprisingly, was a route that would roughly follow the thirty-eighth parallel from central Missouri to the Pacific.

There were many other proposals. In fact, there were so many—each with its own regional advocates—that Congress had debated the question for years before coming up with a scheme that it hoped would solve the dilemma.

On March 2, 1853, Congress passed legislation giving Davis an imaginative but practically impossible mission. The secretary of war was instructed to provide Congress with detailed reports, supported by actual field surveys, of *all* the many proposed routes to the Pacific—within ten months!

Davis quickly mobilized the Corps of Topographical Engineers and sent a series of survey parties west to reconnoiter the several routes. The man chosen to head the survey of the thirty-fifth parallel route, which ran from Fort Smith, Arkansas, through northern Arizona to Los Angeles, was Lieutenant Amiel Weeks Whipple.

The lieutenant was an 1841 graduate of West Point and had been a member of the corps for twelve years. From 1849 to 1852, he had served on the boundary commission that was charged with establishing the border between the United States and Mexico. His primary goal on the thirty-fifth parallel survey was to rechart essentially the same region of Arizona that had been explored by Captain Lorenzo Sitgreaves two years earlier.

Whipple reported positively about the merits of the thirty-fifth parallel route. "There is no doubt remaining that, for the construction of a railway, the route we have passed over is not only practicable but in many respects eminently advantageous," he wrote.

Meanwhile, in anticipation of a transcontinental railroad, the U.S. government had been negotiating with Mexico to buy several million acres of land south of the Gila River. Lieutenant John G. Parke was ordered to begin a survey of the region on December 20,

1853—ten days before Mexican officials sold the land to the United States in a transaction known as the Gadsden Purchase. Parke's survey route generally followed the wagon road laid out by Colonel Philip St. George Cooke in 1846.

Despite the mammoth expense of multiple railroad surveys, nobody paid attention to the engineers' reports when finally they were turned in. Davis anticipated the government's final choice of route when, in 1858, he commented to Congress:

> *With all due respect to my associates, I must say the location of this road will be a political question. It should be a question of engineering, a commercial question, a governmental question—not a question of partisan advantage or of sectional success in a struggle between parties and sections.*

Historian William H. Goetzmann, in his classic study *Army Exploration in the American West 1803–1863,* saw the surveys as an exercise in futility. "Because of miscalculations in their conception, execution, and evaluation," he wrote, "the surveys in fact ultimately became the final stroke of doom to any plan for a federally sponsored transcontinental railroad before the Civil War."

Although the surveys did not have much bearing on the eventual route of the railroad, they did uncover a vast amount of biological, geological, and ethnological data. In fact, this information about relatively unknown regions kept scientists and ethnographers busy for years to come.

Lieutenant Whipple was the namesake of Fort Whipple, established in Arizona in 1863. This army post has more recently served as a Veterans' Administration hospital.

THE GADSDEN PURCHASE

1854

July 15, 1853, found James Gadsden, a sixty-five-year-old native of Charleston, South Carolina, in the office of Secretary of State William L. Marcy. Gadsden, a Yale graduate, former army colonel, and head of a marginally successful railroad company, had been selected by President Franklin Pierce to go to Mexico and resolve the discord that had been growing between the two countries in the five years since the end of the Mexican War.

The primary point of contention was that even after years of meetings, negotiations, and surveys, the two countries could not agree on the boundary line between the Mexican states of Sonora and Chihuahua and what are now New Mexico and Arizona. A six-thousand-square-mile area was being claimed by both countries.

It was not so much the size of the territory that bothered American authorities. Rather, it was the fact that Colonel Philip St. George Cooke's popular wagon road traversed part of it. If the United States did not own the entire route of the wagon road, future American emigrants might have trouble getting to California. In addition, plans were under way for a transcontinental railroad, and one of the proposed routes ran through the contested area.

No one in the United States, Democrat or Whig, was in any mood to go to war with Mexico again. Marcy made it clear that Gadsden was expected to steer the dangerous boundary talks back on course. Gadsden had been highly recommended by the secretary of war, Jefferson Davis, a fellow Southerner who made no secret of his desire to route the transcontinental railroad across the southern part of the country. When Gadsden left Marcy's office, he carried the authority to "pay liberally" for the borderlands required to accommodate the railroad.

Gadsden was in a good position to negotiate when he arrived in Mexico City a year later. General Antonio Lopez de Santa Anna, of Texas Independence and Mexican War fame, had recently returned to power in Mexico and was in the midst of a financial crisis. Mexico needed money far more than it needed land.

Odie B. Faulk described the situation in his book *Destiny Road*.

> *With such moods prevailing in Washington and in Mexico City, both governments were of a mind to remember and accede to the provisions of Article XXI of the Treaty of Guadalupe Hidalgo:*
>
> *"If unhappily any disagreement should hereafter arrive between the Governments of the two Republics . . . they will endeavour in the most sincere and earnest manner, to settle the differences so arising, and to preserve the state of peace and friendship, in which the two countries are now placing themselves."*

After weeks of meetings, Gadsden signed a treaty that he hoped would end the international boundary dispute once and for all. The treaty called for the United States to pay Mexico fifteen million dollars to yield most of the contested area, and it drew the boundary from just north of El Paso, Texas, southwest to the 111th meridian. From there, the border was to turn northwest to the head of the Gulf of California.

The U.S. Senate narrowly failed to ratify the treaty. Instead, it set the boundary where it is today—allowing Mexico to keep more territory—and it cut the payment to Mexico to ten million dollars. Gadsden was so angry that his advice was ignored that he actually lobbied against the revised treaty's passage. However, both countries finally approved it, and on June 29, 1854, the document was signed by President Franklin Pierce.

A new boundary commission was established, with Major William H. Emory, a well-qualified topographical engineer who had ridden with the Army of the West in the Mexican War, serving as the U.S. commissioner. Emory split his survey team into two sections, one to begin its work at El Paso and move westward, and the other to start at Fort Yuma and work eastward. On August 16, 1855, both parties met in the middle, and the long, complicated mission of establishing the international boundary was finally completed. Shortly afterward, Emory met with the Mexican commissioner, Jose Salazar Larregui, and the two pronounced the survey legal.

TROUBLE WITH CAMELS

1857

Edward F. Beale must have pondered ruefully the series of events that had brought him to the eastern bank of the Colorado River on this early fall day in 1857. Beale had been chosen by the War Department to explore and open a wagon road from New Mexico to California. His route would roughly follow that of today's Interstate 40 and would carry him across northern Arizona.

With Beale's party were a number of camels that had been imported into the United States for use in the arid Southwest. As early as 1837, George H. Crosman, a career army officer, had advanced the idea of a camel corps. Eighteen years later, another officer, Henry C. Wayne, had interested Senator Jefferson Davis of Mississippi in the idea. When Davis became secretary of war a couple of years later, he managed to get Congress to appropriate $30,000 for the camel experiment.

About seventy-five camels were purchased in North Africa and the Middle East and shipped to Indianola, Texas. From there, they trekked overland to San Antonio, Fort Stockton, El Paso, and finally

Albuquerque. Beale marched the animals from Albuquerque to Zuni, where the wagon road survey was to begin.

Now Beale watched anxiously as the camels congregated on the Arizona side of the Colorado River. All of the literature he had read indicated that the animals could not swim! How was he going to get this herd, each animal heavily loaded with precious supplies, across the two-hundred-yard-wide, nineteen-foot-deep river without serious consequences?

Beale alluded to his frustrations in an official letter, dated October 18, 1857, to John B. Floyd, the secretary of war.

> *Reading the accounts of travellers who had used them*
> *a great deal in the East, and who, I presumed, were*
> *entirely acquainted with their habits and powers, I*
> *was rendered extremely anxious on the subject of their*
> *swimming; foreseeing that, however useful they might*
> *be as beasts of burden in inhabited parts of the country,*
> *their usefulness would be impaired, if not entirely lost,*
> *to those who desired to use them where ferry boats and*
> *other such conveniences did not exist.*

Beale watched anxiously as the camels strolled up to the riverbank, sniffed the fresh water, and drank for the first time in several days. He was disappointed when the first camel refused to enter the water. He later recalled that,

> *anxious, but not discouraged, I ordered another one*
> *to be brought, one of our largest and finest; and only*
> *those who have felt so much anxiety for the success of*

an experiment can imagine my relief on seeing it take
to the water and swim boldly across the rapidly flowing
river. We then tied them, one to the saddle of another,
and without the slightest difficulty, in a short time
swam them all to the opposite side in gangs. . . . They
not only swam with ease, but with apparently more
strength than horses or mules.

After a journey of forty-eight days, Beale and his crew reached Fort Tejon, California, successfully completing the survey "without an accident of any kind whatsoever." Beale had been as impressed with the beautiful Arizona landscape and the salubrious climate as he had been with the camels. The neighborhood of the San Francisco Peaks was "by far the most beautiful region I ever remember to have seen in any portion of the world," he wrote.

Beale and his camels returned to the East via the same route in early 1858. Still, for reasons never fully explained, the War Department viewed the camel experiment as a failure. Eventually, it decided to dispose of the animals. Beale had meanwhile acquired a huge ranch in California. When word reached him that the camels were being sold, he purchased most of the herd and resettled the animals on his spread.

Beale went on to become surveyor-general of California and Nevada and U.S. minister to Austria-Hungary. He died in Washington, D.C., in 1893, at the age of seventy-one.

THE BRIEF SUCCESS OF THE OVERLAND MAIL

1858

John Butterfield was a man of vision. From humble beginnings as a New York stagecoach driver, he had built a successful mail service in that state, increasing his fortune along the way. He was also prominent in real estate and banking circles, and at one time he served as mayor of Utica, New York.

But it is not for his success as a New York politician and businessman that Butterfield is remembered today. Rather, his fame stems from his organization and leadership of the Overland Mail Company.

In the late 1850s, California was still a remote outpost of the United States. Although the region's population had grown significantly since statehood in 1850, an enormous distance separated it from the East. There were only three ways to cross that distance: First, there was the long, difficult overland journey, which could take weeks or even months. Second, there was the sea journey from an eastern port to Central America, then overland across Panama or

Nicaragua, and then by sea again up the coast to California. And finally, there was the sea journey around the tip of South America. Obviously, none of the routes provided a timely way of transporting the U.S. mail.

In March 1857, Congress passed legislation authorizing the creation of an overland mail service. Bids were let to various entrepreneurs, and in September the contract was awarded to the Overland Mail Company, an establishment formed by John Butterfield and several associates. For $600,000 a year, the firm agreed to provide mail service twice a week from Memphis and St. Louis to San Francisco and Los Angeles. The contract required that each delivery be completed in less than twenty-five days.

For the next year, the Overland Mail Company spent more than a million dollars exploring a route, building way stations, buying coaches and equipment, and hiring drivers and other employees. Finally, on September 14, 1853, the first mail run started cross-country from San Francisco. It arrived in St. Louis twenty-four days, eighteen hours, and twenty-six minutes later. In the meantime, the westbound run had left St. Louis on September 16. It arrived in San Francisco in twenty-three days, twenty-three hours, and thirty minutes.

In Arizona, the Overland Mail Company route followed much of the earlier wagon road blazed by Colonel Philip St. George Cooke. The primary difference was that the mail route entered Arizona from New Mexico several miles farther north, to take advantage of Apache Pass. The trail passed through Tucson and then turned north, generally following the Gila River to its confluence with the Colorado at Yuma.

Way stations along the route were about twenty miles apart. Those in Arizona were built of stone or adobe. Each station was manned by about six to eight employees whose duties were to care for the horses and mules and to be sure a fresh team was ready for the stage when it arrived. For the comfort of any passengers who might be aboard, a fresh coach was provided every three hundred miles.

Butterfield's motto was "Remember boys, nothing on God's earth must stop the United States mail." To live up to his maxim, he hired only the best men for the job and bought only the best livestock available. According to Waterman L. Ormsby, a correspondent at the time for the New York *Herald*, Butterfield's employees were without exception "courteous, civil, and attentive." Most of them were from the East, he noted, and many were from New York. "I found the drivers on the whole, fine and with few exceptions experienced men," he said. "All the superintendents are experienced men."

Of the horses that pulled the heavy coaches, Ormsby wrote, "[They] are of the most powerful description to be found, and when once thoroughly trained to the service perform the laborious run with apparent pleasure and delight." In Arizona, mules were usually substituted for the horses because they were better suited to the terrain.

The Overland Mail Company employed close to two thousand men and operated about two hundred way stations along its 2,800-mile route between the Mississippi River and the Pacific Ocean. With the onset of the Civil War, the company closed its southern road and shifted most of its activity farther north.

The Overland Mail Company was one of the most massive undertakings of its time. However, despite strong financial backing, brilliant leadership, and excellent planning, it was doomed to fail. It was simply too big and too expensive. By the time Butterfield was replaced as company chairman in 1860, the rival Pony Express had made its debut. Telegraph lines and railroad tracks would soon span the continent. The Overland Mail Company was a victim of progress.

THE CONFEDERATE
CONQUEST OF ARIZONA

1862

When Captain Sherrod Hunter entered Tucson on February 28, 1862, in command of two hundred "Arizona Volunteers," he was cheered by the largely pro-Southern residents of the town. Hunter was part of General Henry Hopkins Sibley's Confederate Army of New Mexico. He had been ordered to California by his commander, and the stopover at Tucson was for rest and new supplies.

Hunter probably did not realize that Tucson and much of the surrounding region had been officially declared the Territory of Arizona by the Confederate Congress in Richmond, Virginia, only a month earlier. The new territory comprised all of present-day New Mexico and Arizona south of the thirty-fourth parallel.

But even before the official creation of a Confederate Arizona Territory, there had been an unofficial one. It had been the dream of John Robert Baylor since 1861.

Baylor, a Kentucky-born, Texas-raised Indian fighter, had been a key player in persuading the Texas government to secede from the Union in March 1861. When he was assured of Texas secession, Baylor recruited a large party of neighbors and friends to join him in a much-publicized "buffalo hunt" in West Texas. But the hunt was merely a cover-up for an invasion of New Mexico and Arizona.

Baylor was a lieutenant colonel of the Confederacy's Second Regiment of Texas Mounted Volunteers. He and his "buffalo hunters" quickly occupied Fort Bliss, Texas, and poised for an attack on Fort Fillmore, New Mexico. In late July, his men entered the town of Mesilla, just outside Fort Fillmore. When Union troops from the fort marched upon Mesilla demanding a Confederate surrender, the Texas troops so overpowered them that Baylor captured the entire Union command.

The following week, Baylor declared himself governor of the "Territory of Arizona," and named Mesilla as its capital. He was quick to justify his actions.

> *The social and political condition of Arizona being little short of general anarchy, and the people literally destitute of law, order and protection, the said Territory from the date hereof, is hereby declared temporarily organized as a military government, until such time as [the Confederate] Congress may otherwise provide.*

Everyone but the Union Army and the Indians was happy. The Confederate high command was pleased because Baylor's self-styled territory included the trail to California, the control of which was much desired by the South. The Americans who lived in Tucson, Mesilla, and most of the other villages in the territory were mostly displaced Southerners to begin with.

The Apaches were a different story. They had been on the war-path since 1861, when a young Army lieutenant, George N. Bascom, tried to capture Cochise at Apache Pass. To the chagrin of the Southerners, the Apaches made no distinction between Union and Confederate troops. By spring of 1862, the Indians held the entire Confederate Territory of Arizona hostage, and there was little that either the Union or the Confederate army could do.

Temporarily putting his war with the Union aside, Colonel Baylor turned his attention to the Apaches. Baylor intensely disliked Indians, and on March 20 he made those feelings clear in orders he issued to a captain of the Arizona Guards, a loosely organized group of about thirty volunteers.

> *You will . . . use all means to persuade the Apaches or any tribe to come in for the purpose of making peace, and when you get them together kill all the grown Indians and take the children prisoners and sell them to defray the expense of killing the Indians. Buy whiskey and such other goods as may be necessary for the Indians and I will order vouchers given to cover the amount expended. Leave nothing undone to insure success, and have a sufficient number of men around to allow no Indians to escape.*

Fortunately for the Apaches and their allies, Baylor's unconscionable plan was interrupted by an unexpected development within the Confederate command. General Henry H. Sibley had arrived in El Paso in December 1861 and had asserted authority over all Confederate troops in the West. He made it clear that his move was not intended to "abrogate or supersede the powers of Col. John R.

Baylor, as civil and military governor of Arizona." Nevertheless, the presence of a Confederate officer of higher rank, whose priority was the final conquest and occupation of *all* of the federally recognized New Mexico Territory, more or less placed Baylor's schemes on the back burner.

Sibley attacked Union-occupied Fort Craig, and then defeated Colonel Edward R. S. Canby at the Battle of Valverde on February 21, 1862. Quickly following up on his victory, he marched on Albuquerque and Santa Fe and easily took both towns. In late March, at Glorieta Pass, about twenty miles southeast of Santa Fe, Sibley's forces met a combined army of Union regulars and Colorado volunteers. After three days of intense fighting, during which the Confederates lost all their wagons and supplies, Sibley's defeated army began a long retreat to Texas.

As it turned out, there was to be no lasting Confederate Territory of Arizona and no permanent Southern occupation of New Mexico. When Sibley's forces left New Mexico after the Battle of Glorieta Pass, the Union kept control of the region for the duration of the Civil War.

KIT CARSON'S VICTORY
OVER THE NAVAJOS

1864

In the early 1860s, Apache and Navajo warriors resentful of white encroachment on traditional Indian lands were launching bloody raids against Arizona's vulnerable new settlers. Union General James Henry Carleton had no intention of allowing the attacks to go unchecked. As his self-proclaimed "California Column" marched into Tucson on a hot day in May 1862, he knew exactly how he planned to deal with the Indians.

Carleton was a captain at the outbreak of the Civil War, but within a year he had climbed to the rank of colonel, and eventually he was promoted to general. He was assigned command of the two thousand or so members of the California Column in late 1861. A career soldier, Carleton had served with distinction in the Mexican War, and at one time he was the commandant of Fort Union, New Mexico. He was stationed in California and was commander of the military district for the southern part of that state when he was ordered to retake New Mexico and Arizona from the Confederates, who had just seized control of this region they now called the Territory of Arizona.

On June 8, 1862, in the town of Tucson, Carleton declared himself military governor of Arizona. In an address to the local residents, he said:

> *In the present chaotic state in which Arizona is to be found: with no civil officers to administer the laws: indeed with an utter absence of all civil authority: and with no security of life or property within its borders: it becomes the duty of the undersigned to represent the authority of the United States.*

In late July, Carleton left Union troops to guard Tucson and marched toward the Rio Grande to engage a Confederate force led by General Henry Hopkins Sibley. Two advance units of Carleton's army had already skirmished with Apaches at Apache Pass, near the New Mexico border. In a separate incident, a third unit had opened fire on an Apache party with artillery, chasing the Indians off—at least temporarily.

As Carleton's California Column approached, Sibley's troops, recently defeated at the Battle of Glorieta Pass, retreated to Texas, leaving Carleton with no enemy to fight. So he turned his attention to the Indians of the region.

The Apaches and Navajos both had long histories of hostility, particularly toward the earlier Mexican inhabitants of the region. After the arrival of whites in the area, however, it did not take long for the Indians to turn their aggression upon the newcomers.

Carleton's recipe for dealing with Indians was simple—and similar to that of many other military and civilian leaders of the time. He wanted their complete submission and their transfer to reservations. As more and more reports of Indian-white confrontations reached him during late 1862 and early 1863, he set his plan in action.

By spring of 1863, Carleton's New Mexico Volunteers, led by Kit Carson, had just about defeated the Mescalero Apaches. Most of the Indians had been sent off to a new reservation along the Pecos River called Bosque Redondo. As Carleton began his Navajo campaign, he relied on Carson yet again. He had every intention of sending the Navajo tribe to the new reservation as well.

Desultory fighting continued throughout the summer of 1863. Finally, Carleton lost all patience and ordered Carson to tell the Navajos to

> *go to the Bosque Redondo, or we will pursue and destroy you. We will not make peace with you on any other terms. You have deceived us too often and robbed and murdered our people too long to trust you again at large in your own country. This war shall be pursued against you if it takes years, now that we have begun, until you cease to exist or move. There can be no other talk on the subject.*

The Navajo Nation was defeated in early January 1864, when Kit Carson and almost four hundred men marched on the traditional Navajo stronghold of Canyon de Chelly. After a brisk fight, the Navajos counted twenty-three dead, five wounded, and more than two hundred captured. Additionally, two hundred head of goats and sheep had been commandeered, and many crops and fruit orchards had been destroyed. A proud Carleton wrote U.S. Adjutant General Lorenzo Thomas on February 7, 1864.

> *This is the first time any troops, whether when the country belonged to Mexico or since we acquired it,*

*have been able to pass through the Canon de Chelly.
. . . It has been the great fortress of the tribe since time
out of mind. To this point they fled when pressed by
our troops. Colonel Washington, Colonel Sumner,
and many other commanders have made an attempt
to go through it, but had to retrace their steps. It was
reserved for Colonel Carson to be the first to succeed.
. . .*

*I believe this will be the last Navajo war. The
persistent efforts which have been and will continue
to be made can hardly fail to bring in the whole tribe
before the year ends. I beg respectfully to call the serious
attention of the government to the destitute condition
of the captives, and beg for authority to provide clothing for the women and children. Every preparation
will be made to plant large crops for their subsistence
at the Bosque Redondo the coming spring. Whether
the Indian department will do anything for these Indians or not you will know. But whatever is to be done
should be done at once. At all events, as I before wrote
to you, "we can feed them cheaper than we can fight
them."*

In the days following Carson's siege of Canyon de Chelly, almost
eight thousand Navajo men, women, and children were forcibly
marched to the Bosque Redondo reservation. The scene must have
been reminiscent of the infamous "Trail of Tears," the forced march
inflicted on the Cherokees a quarter of a century earlier.

POWELL'S GRAND CANYON ADVENTURE

1869

The date was August 13, 1869, and Major John Wesley Powell, a former Union artillery officer who had lost his right arm at the Battle of Shiloh, was about to depart on a journey that he had dreamed of for the past two years. Powell, a geologist and ethnographer, had camped overnight with nine companions at the mouth of the Little Colorado River. As dawn broke, he wrote in his journal:

> *We are now ready to start on our way down the Great Unknown. Our boats, tied to a common stake, chafe each other as they are tossed by the fretful river. They ride high and buoyant, for their loads are lighter than we could desire. We have but a month's rations remaining. The flour has been resifted through the mosquito-net sieve; the spoiled bacon has been dried and the worst of it boiled; the few pounds of dried*

apples have been spread in the sun and reshrunken to
their normal bulk. The sugar has all melted and gone
on its way down the river. But we have a large sack of
coffee. The lightening of the boats has this advantage:
they will ride the waves better and we shall have but
little to carry when we make a portage.

Powell and his friends were about to enter the Grand Canyon, the last leg of a trip that had begun on May 24, 1869, on the Green River in present-day Wyoming. Powell's dream was to become the first white man to float down the Green to the Colorado and then through the Grand Canyon to the Virgin River.

The party left the town of Green River with four boats, three of them "built of oak; stanch [*sic*] and firm; double-ribbed, with double stem and stern posts, and further strengthened by bulkheads. . . ." The fourth was built of pine, "very light . . . and every way built for fast rowing. . . ." Supplies of all kinds filled all four boats, including clothing, food, traps, axes, hammers, nails and screws, firearms, and ammunition. Since Powell's expedition was scientific in nature—in fact, it was sponsored by the Smithsonian Institution—barometers, thermometers, chronometers, compasses, and other delicate instruments were included.

Two and a half months after leaving Green River, Powell and his company finally arrived at the entrance of the Grand Canyon. There, at the bottom of the chasm, Powell contemplated the expedition's future.

We have an unknown distance yet to run, an unknown
river to explore. What falls there are, we know not;
what rocks beset the channel, we know not; what walls

rise over the river, we know not. Ah, well! we may con-
jecture many things. The men talk as cheerfully as ever;
jests are bandied about freely this morning; but to me
the cheer is somber and the jests are ghastly.

As the expedition made its way down the rapid and treacherous
Colorado, the cliffs that dwarfed the men and their boats seemed to
reach ever higher to the sky. Powell lamented:

The walls now are more than a mile in height. . . .
Stand on the south steps of the Treasury building in
Washington and look down Pennsylvania Avenue to
the Capitol; measure this distance overhead, and imag-
ine cliffs to extend to that altitude, and you will under-
stand what is meant.

For the next several days, Powell's expedition endured both
rough water and a drenching rain. Most of their supplies were gone,
all of the remaining food was spoiled, and the men were exhausted
from their constant combat with the rapids. Then, on the evening
of August 27, Powell had to make the most important decision of
the entire journey. Three of his men thought it was sheer nonsense
to continue down the river by boat. They decided to leave the main
party and trek overland to civilization. Powell labored with his con-
science all night. He wrote:

I almost conclude to leave the river. But for years I
have been contemplating this trip. To leave the explo-
ration unfinished, to say that there is a part of the

canyon which I cannot explore, having already nearly accomplished it, is more than I am willing to acknowledge, and I determine to go on.

At noon two days later, Powell and the remaining expedition members exited the Grand Canyon. Powell described their elation in his journal.

The relief from danger and the joy of success are great. . . . Now the danger is over, now the toil has ceased, now the gloom has disappeared, now the firmament is bounded only by the horizon, and what a vast expanse of constellations can be seen!

Powell explored the Grand Canyon again the following year, and in future years he was involved in several other explorations in the American West. When Congress authorized the Bureau of Ethnology as a branch of the Smithsonian Institution in 1879, Powell was selected as its first director, a post he held until his death in 1902.

THE CAMP GRANT MASSACRE

1871

From the earliest intrusion of whites into their territory, the Apache Indians had tried to maintain friendly relations with them. In fact, the Indians so despised their Mexican neighbors that they would have gladly allied themselves with the Americans just to annihilate those traditional enemies. One of the earliest indications of what could have been a beautiful relationship between the two cultures occurred on October 20, 1846, at an encampment of General Stephen Watts Kearny's Army of the West near the Gila River. Major William H. Emory described the scene in his official government report.

> The general sent word to the Apaches he would not start [the meeting] till 9 or 10. This gave them time to come in, headed by their chief, Red Sleeve [Mangas Coloradas]. They swore eternal friendship to the whites, and everlasting hatred to the Mexicans. The Indians said that . . . white men might now pass in

safety through their country; that if they were hungry, they would feed them; or, if on foot, mount them. . . . One of the chiefs, after eyeing the general with apparent great admiration, broke out in a vehement manner: "You have taken New Mexico, and will soon take California; go, then, and take Chihuahua, Durango, and Sonora. We will help you. You fight for land; we care nothing for land; we fight for the laws of Montezuma and for food. The Mexicans are rascals; we hate and will kill them all."

As years passed, however, this benevolence of the Apache leadership faded, hastened no doubt by the ill treatment meted out by the newcomers. Several years later, John C. Cremony, who had served as an interpreter for the Boundary Commission from 1849 to 1851, squarely placed the blame for poor Apache-white relations on lack of understanding on the whites' part. He wrote:

Our Government has expended millions of dollars, in driblets, since the acquisition of California, in efforts to reduce the Apaches and Navajoes [sic], who occupy that extensive belt of country which forms the highway for overland migration from East to the West; but we are as far from success to-day as we were twenty years ago. The reason is obvious. We have never striven to make ourselves intelligently acquainted with those tribes. Nearly all that relates to them is quite as uncertain and indefinite to our comprehension as that which obtains in the center of Africa. Those who were the best informed on the matter, and had given it the closest attention, were, at the same time—most unfortunately—the least capable of imparting their information; while those who were almost ignorant of the subject have been the most forward to give the results of their fragmentary gleanings.

As guilty as misunderstanding and lack of realistic information were, plain old hatred took the forefront in many of the confrontations between whites and Apaches. And there is no doubt that hatred played the primary role in an episode that occurred at Camp Grant on April 30, 1871—one of the most shocking, bloodthirsty, and unconscionable chapters in the history of Arizona.

It all started in February and March 1871, when Lieutenant Royal E. Whitman, the commander at Camp Grant, agreed to house and feed several hundred poor, homeless Apaches who had no place else to go. Whitman settled the Indians in a temporary camp half a mile from his post and issued them rations every other day, while carefully explaining to them that he would need approval from higher authority to continue this arrangement. Whitman's letter to General George Stoneman, the officer in charge of all of Arizona, requesting further advice and instructions was returned after six weeks with no reply and no indication that Stoneman had even seen it.

In the meantime, a Captain Frank Stanwood arrived at Camp Grant with verbal instructions from General Stoneman "to recognize and feed any Indians he might find at the post as 'prisoners of war.'" Satisfying himself that all was in order with Whitman's Apache charges, Stanwood left on patrol on April 24. Whitman was happy that affairs were going so well. He wrote:

Such was the condition of things up to the morning of the thirtieth of April. They had so won on me, that from my first idea of treating them justly and honestly as an officer of the Army, I had come to feel a strong personal interest in helping to show them the way to a higher civilization. I had come to feel respect for men who, ignorant and naked, were still ashamed to lie or steal, for women who would work cheerfully like slaves to clothe themselves and children, but untaught, held their virtue above price.

Whitman's well-being was shattered on the morning of April 30 when he was advised by messenger that a party of well-armed citizens had left Tucson on April 28, in the company of more than one hundred Mexicans and Tohono O'odham, intending to raid the nearby Apache village and kill its inhabitants. When attempts were made to warn the Apaches and to bring them into the protection of the fort, it was too late. A heartsick Whitman wrote of the disaster.

My messengers returned in about an hour, with intelligence that they could find no living Indians. The camp was burning and the ground strewed with their dead and mutilated women and children. I immediately mounted a party of about twenty soldiers and citizens, and sent them with the post surgeon, with a wagon to bring in the wounded, if any could be found. The party returned late in the P. M., having found no wounded and without having been able to communicate with any of the survivors. Early the next morning

I took a similar party, with spades and shovels, and went out and buried all the dead in and immediately about the camp. . . . While at the work many of them [the Apache survivors] came to the spot and indulged in their expressions of grief, too wild and terrible to be described.

The massacre at Camp Grant had been perpetrated by some of Tucson's leading citizens, including the former mayor, the owner of the newspaper, and a former member of the territorial legislature. They called themselves the Tucson Committee of Public Safety, and they accused the Indians sheltered at Camp Grant of leaving the post periodically to raid the surrounding countryside, leaving a trail of blood in their wake. The accusation, unfortunately, was entirely unfounded.

BILLY THE KID'S FIRST MURDER

1877

Friday, August 17, 1877, dawned hot and dry, just like most summer days in southeastern Arizona. Several people had gathered outside the local cantina in the tiny village of Bonita, not far from the U.S. army post, Camp Grant. In the midst of the growing crowd, two men were exchanging heated words.

One of the men was Frank P. Cahill, a large-framed Irishman about thirty-two years old. The other was a short, slightly built, bucktoothed boy who was going by the name of Henry Antrim. Sometimes he called himself Henry McCarty. Everyone at Camp Grant just called him the Kid.

Although most of the bystanders couldn't hear what the two men were saying, they could tell that the conversation was getting serious. Cahill and the Kid grappled with each other, and then, quick as a flash, the Kid pulled a pistol and fired. Cahill grabbed his stomach and slumped to the ground. A few friends carried the big Irishman into the cantina and tried to minister to his gaping wound.

What happened next isn't entirely clear. One account reported that the Kid was arrested and that he later escaped. Another said he simply rode off unchallenged. One fact is certain, however. Although his victim didn't die until the next day, Billy the Kid had just killed his first man.

Almost a week later, the local newspaper, the *Arizona Weekly Star,* reported the incident.

> *Frank P. Cahill was shot by Henry Antrim alias the Kid at Camp Grant on the 17th, and died on the 18th. The following are the dying words of the deceased:*
>
> *I Frank P. Cahill, being convinced that I am about to die, do make the following as my final statement: My name is Frank P. Cahill. I was born in the county and town of Galway, Ireland. Yesterday, Aug. 17th, 1877, I had some trouble with Henry Antrem [sic], otherwise known as the Kid, during which time he shot me. I had called him a pimp, and he called me a s— of a b—, we then took hold of each other; I did not hit him, I think; saw him go for his pistol, and tried to get hold of it, but could not and he shot me in the belly.*

This was not the first time the eighteen-year-old Kid had been in trouble with the law around Camp Grant. He had arrived at the army post from New Mexico the previous year. Working on local ranches as a cowboy, he sometimes supplemented his meager income by gambling and herding stolen horses. He got into serious trouble in late 1876, when he stole a horse belonging to a cavalryman named Sergeant Louis Hartman. The sergeant went after the Kid with four other soldiers, recovered the horse, but found that he had no authority to arrest a civilian. In the next several months, the Kid was arrested twice for horse theft, but he escaped from jail both times. Nevertheless, he remained in the Camp Grant neighborhood until the following August, when he killed Cahill.

Probably no other outlaw in American history is as widely known as Billy the Kid. Yet, some of his past is still shrouded in mystery. He apparently was born in New York City in 1859, the son of Patrick and Catherine Devine McCarty. After Patrick died, in about 1864, the family moved to Wichita, Kansas, and later, in 1873, to Santa Fe, New Mexico. There, Catherine married William H. Antrim. While in New Mexico, the Kid started using the alias William Bonney, for reasons unknown.

Much has been written about Billy the Kid in the past century— not all of it true. Pat Garrett, the sheriff who killed Billy in New Mexico in 1881, left one account of the legendary outlaw's youth. In the book, *The Authentic Life of Billy, the Kid,* published in Santa Fe in 1882, Garrett wrote of the Kid in glowing terms.

He exhibited no characteristics prophecying [sic] his desperate and disastrous future. Bold, daring, and reckless, he was open-handed, generous-hearted, frank, and manly. He was a favorite with all classes and ages, especially was he loved and admired by the old and decrepit, and the young and helpless. To such he was a champion, a defender, a benefactor, a right arm. He was never seen to accost a lady, especially an elderly one, but with his hat in his hand, and did her attire or appearance evidence poverty, it was a poem to see the eager, sympathetic, deprecating look in Billy's sunny face, as he proffered assistance or afforded information.

More recent writers have not been so kind to Billy. The eminent western historian Jeff Dykes once called the Kid "that mythical hero, the Robin Hood of the Southwest, who was once just a buck-toothed, thieving, murderous, little cowboy-gone-bad."

Whether Billy was really a "cowboy-gone-bad" or rotten from the start is a question that will be debated for as long as the Old West is remembered. One thing is certain, however. As a young man, the Kid courted trouble wherever he went. When he left Camp Grant, he returned to New Mexico and became involved in the Lincoln County War. It was shortly after that melee that Garrett caught up with him and shot him dead at Pete Maxwell's ranch in Fort Sumner, New Mexico. A lawless career was over, and a legend was born.

THE APATHETIC REIGN
OF JOHN FREMONT

1878

In late September 1878, three men, three women, and a staghound climbed off a train at Fort Yuma, California. The soldiers at the fort paid little attention to the newcomers, who were all decked out in Eastern attire. But it became clear they were no ordinary travelers when the commandant of the fort personally appeared to offer them overland transportation to Prescott, Arizona. The soldiers watched with increased interest as General John Charles Fremont, the newly appointed governor of the Arizona Territory; his wife, Jessie; their grown children, Lily and Frank; and two servants, Mary and Ah Chung, set off for their new home.

Fremont's name had been on the tip of everyone's tongue in the 1840s, when he had led several explorations into the vast wilderness of the American West. He was still popular in 1856, when he ran for president on the new Republican Party ticket. And he served a tour of duty as a general during the Civil War.

But by the 1870s, Fremont's explorations were ancient history. His presidential bid had failed miserably, and his military career had been unimpressive (a modern historian called him "one of the North's greatest military embarrassments"). Fremont and his family were not only largely forgotten but nearly destitute as well.

Jessie Fremont was the one who kept bread on the table during those lean years. She was the daughter of Thomas Hart Benton, one of the nation's most powerful senators during the early years of westward expansion. She was also a writer, and the income from her magazine articles and books rescued the family more than once when her husband's wild get-rich schemes failed.

In 1877, the Fremonts lost their house on Madison Avenue in New York City and moved to rental property on Staten Island. They were nearly ruined financially. They even had to sell many valuable and sentimental paintings and pieces of furniture and china. In a last ditch effort to save themselves, John and Jessie traveled to Washington, D.C., in the spring of 1878 to see John's old friend and admirer Rutherford B. Hayes, who had recently been elected president.

Out of this providential meeting came Fremont's appointment to the governorship of the Arizona Territory. Although the salary was only $2,600 a year, John and Jessie believed this would be a new beginning. Happily, they prepared to leave New York for California. From there, they would proceed to their new post at Prescott.

The 230-mile trip from Fort Yuma to Prescott was long and tiring. For eight days, the Fremonts rumbled across hot, featureless desert in mule-drawn army ambulances. Eventually, they rented a home in Prescott for ninety dollars a month, quite a bite out of John's $217-a-month salary. To save money, Jessie, Lily, and Mary cleaned and redecorated the house themselves.

Governor Fremont's attention quickly wandered from territorial affairs and centered instead on the recent flurry of gold and silver strikes in the area. He soon succumbed to yet another bout of "get-rich-quick fever." With a territorial supreme court judge as his partner, the governor inspected several mining properties and then, in February 1879, headed East to lure prospective investors. His apparent lack of interest in territorial matters did not go unnoticed by members of the legislature.

Fremont returned to Arizona in August. He had succeeded in interesting a group of investors and wasted no time in searching for appropriate mining properties. Jessie journeyed to New York herself in November, believing that if her husband really did hit it big, he would need representation among the investors. While there, she confided to one of the investment group that her husband really wanted to leave his position as governor, "but to resign now would give the power next winter when the Legislature meets again, to unknown people and interests." By staying in office a little longer, she added, John would be able to "prevent and veto any vexatious legislation regarding mines and railroads."

John joined Jessie in New York in March 1880, and the two aggressively promoted their mining scheme, as well as plans for a cattle ranch and a railroad.

Returning to Arizona in October was a necessary evil for Fremont, since he had to attend to territorial business. He moved to Tucson in March 1881 and almost immediately was off to New York again. More machinations in New York throughout the year left Fremont precious little time to worry about his official duties in Arizona. His perpetual absence from and apparent disinterest in the territory was obvious to both his associates there and to his superiors in Washington. The governor resembled "a hen on a hot griddle, popping from Arizona to New York and Washington . . . in a bewildering manner," one dissatisfied observer reported. By the time most of the Fremonts' financial schemes failed, the new president, Chester Arthur, had recalled John from Arizona.

Fremont's forced resignation was effective October 11, 1881. The Fremonts lived out their lives in comparative poverty in New York, supported primarily by Jessie's writing.

Shortly before John's death in 1890, he was given an honorary promotion to major-general so that he could receive a military pension. Jessie died in 1902.

Fremont could boast of few achievements while governor of the Arizona Territory. Yet, despite his long absences and other interests, he did find some time to spend on government matters. Most of the issues for which he lobbied involved trade between Arizona and New Mexico, development of mining resources, water reclamation, and transportation improvement.

The eminent western historian Hubert Howe Bancroft probably summed up Fremont's tenure in Arizona as well as anybody. He wrote that John was "appointed merely that his chronic poverty might be relieved; and in Arizona he seems to have done nothing worse than neglect his duties."

THE DEBUT OF
THE TOMBSTONE EPITAPH

1880

"Tombstone is a city set upon a hill, promising to vie with ancient Rome, upon her seven hills, in a fame different in character but no less in importance," exclaimed the premier issue of *The Tombstone Epitaph* on May 1, 1880. Like all fledgling towns in the American West, Tombstone had been quick to support a newspaper of its own. And the newspaper was quick to sing the praises of the community it aimed to serve.

> *Scarcely a year has passed since the limits of the townsite were proclaimed and the hardy pioneer settler raised the first structure of human abode. To-day Tombstone affords over 500 roofs for the shelter of man and beast, with a population of about four to each of the aforesaid sheltering roofs. To this sturdy, prosperous population and the public in general—on*

*this bright, brand new May morning, our natal day,
the first May morning in the new decade of 1880—
the EPITAPH [ex]tends a hearty and cordial greet-
ing. No tombstone is complete without its epitaph,
and so we have come to fill the void and make all
happy in the consequent perfection.*

The founder of the *Epitaph* was John P. Clum, who in addition
to editing the newspaper in its early days, served as one of the town's
early mayors. Born in 1851 in upper New York State, the versatile
Clum dabbled in many professions before he died, among them lawyer, preacher, actor, teacher, and politician. As a young man, Clum
migrated West with the army. In late 1873, he was appointed Indian
agent to the San Carlos Apache Indian Reservation in the Arizona
Territory. He began the job almost a year later, after spending time
in Washington, D.C., learning his new responsibilities.

Within weeks of arriving at the San Carlos Agency, Clum had
whipped affairs into order. In December, he wrote to a friend that
he had already provided for

*a clerk, a farmer, a mason, a carpenter, a blacksmith,
an interpreter, a priest, a cook, a physician, a teacher
and several (white) laborers. I also employ from ten to
100 Indians daily. . . . This was considered one of the
worst of agencies, but I would not now exchange it for
any other.*

During Clum's tenure at San Carlos, the infamous Apache chief
Geronimo was the most active renegade in the territory. His constant
raids on farmers and ranchers in Arizona, as well as his hit-and-run

attacks on Mexican villages in Sonora, were a source of perpetual fear and anxiety. As Indian agent, Clum once captured the wily and elusive Apache chief, but Geronimo was later released. Wallace E. Clayton, the current editor of *The Tombstone Epitaph*, wrote in 1980 that

> *Clum recommended Geronimo be hanged for his murders at the time of his capture. Had the advice been followed, five hundred lives and $12 million would have been saved, for this was the toll of the Geronimo raids during the Apache Wars of 1882–1886.*

The first issue of the *Epitaph* was four pages long, and its front-page story covered the recent silver finds in the vicinity. The discovery in 1877 of silver in the area was what prompted the settlement of Tombstone to begin with. At least five mines were established, all with fanciful names: the Good Enough, Tough Nut, Westside, Defense, and Surveyor. Within three years, the newspaper reported, almost half a million dollars worth of silver bars had been stamped from the rich ore extracted from the mines.

In closing his article about the fabulous wealth the silver mines were bringing to the infant community of Tombstone, Clum poetically wrote:

> *We are glad that we were not beloved by the gods,*
> *for we might have then died young, and though our*
> *epitaph might have been chiseled on the purest Italian marble, we would much prefer that it should be*
> *graven in carbonate [silver ore] and are thankful that*
> *our feet have been permitted to traverse the levels of*

*this metallic cryptogram and our eyes to dwell upon the
extensive silver wealth of one of the finest mining properties on the Pacific Coast.*

The first issue of the *Epitaph* also featured a variety of paid
advertisements heralding everything from G. F. Spangenberg's
gunsmithing shop "in Tin Shop, Fourth st., near Post Office," to
Tasker's & Pridham's general merchandise emporium, which sold,
among other things,

> *Staple Dry Goods and Groceries, Gent's Furnishing
> Goods, Clothing, Boots and Shoes. Also, a Full Line
> of Miners' and Builders' Hardware, Agricultural
> Tools, Nails, Etc. Also, a Full Assortment of WINES,
> LIQUORS, and CIGARS. Our stock of Imported and
> Domestic Wines, Liquors and Cigars comprise all the
> Choicest Brands in the market and can not be excelled
> in any house in Arizona.*

After a couple of years in Tombstone, Clum moved on to California, then to Washington, D.C., and finally to Alaska, where he
served a stint as postal inspector during the Klondike gold rush of
1898. He died of a heart attack on May 2, 1932, just short of his
eighty-first birthday.

THE GUNFIGHT AT THE OK CORRAL

1881

October 26, 1881, was a typical Wednesday in the booming mining town of Tombstone. Men and women scurried up and down Fremont Street on their daily errands, while a few lazy dogs stretched out along the plank sidewalk in front of the barbershop. Inside, the town's sheriff, John Behan, was getting a shave. As the barber finished lathering his face, someone bolted through the door with news that the Clantons and the Earps were in town. A shootout between the two groups seemed imminent.

Behan hastily wiped his face clean and hurried down Fremont Street to a vacant lot behind the OK Corral. A small crowd of men was gathered there: Ike Clanton, his brother Billy, brothers Tom and Frank McLaury, and Billy Claiborne. Behan noticed that only Frank McLaury and Billy Clanton were armed, and when he asked them to turn in their weapons, they said they were just about to leave town.

Just then, Behan saw the Earp brothers—Wyatt, Virgil, and Morgan—coming down Fremont along with John H. (Doc) Holliday. Behan tried to tell the foursome that the Clantons and

McLaurys were unarmed, but he was shoved brusquely aside. What happened next was the birth of a legend.

For about a minute, guns blazed. When the smoke cleared, a few wary spectators found Frank McLaury, his brother Tom, and Billy Clanton lying dead. Virgil and Morgan Earp had been wounded in the leg and neck respectively. Billy Claiborne and Ike Clanton, unarmed and unable to protect themselves, had run away. Wyatt Earp and Doc Holliday emerged from the shootout unscathed.

Wyatt Earp has always been considered the hero of the shootout at the OK Corral, primarily because of an account of the incident in an inaccurate and biased biography written by a friend, Stuart N. Lake (*Wyatt Earp: Frontier Marshal*). Numerous off-base television shows and movies have perpetuated Earp's reputation. Even today, after historians have spent decades debunking the myth of the man and his role in Tombstone history, he still rides high among the uninformed as a great hero of the American West.

In fact, Wyatt Earp was nothing more than a part-time lawman who made most of his living by gambling and who was not adverse to breaking the law himself if it was to his advantage. At the time of the shootout, Earp's brother Virgil was the town marshal, and he had deputized Wyatt, Morgan, and Doc Holliday. They were responsible for keeping order within the town limits. Behan and his deputies upheld the laws of the newly established Cochise County.

The Clanton gang was known as the "Cowboys." They had been led by Newman H. ("Old Man") Clanton, the father of Billy and Ike, until Newman's death the previous August. They were known to rustle Mexican cattle for resale in Arizona. Illegal though this activity was, it should not have concerned the town marshals of Tombstone.

In reality, the Earps had come gunning for the Clantons and their friends because Ike Clanton knew that Wyatt and Doc Holliday were the perpetrators of a recent stagecoach robbery. Earp had already tried bribery. He had offered Clanton the reward money if Clanton would permanently silence any talk of the actual robbers.

No one will ever know exactly what sparked the famous gunfight at the OK Corral. In a written explanation, Wyatt Earp blamed the entire affair on the Clantons.

> *They—Billy Clanton and Frank McLowery [sic] commenced to draw their pistols; at the same time Tom McLowery threw his hand to his hip and jumped behind a horse. I had my pistol in my overcoat pocket where I had put it when Behan told me he had disarmed the other party. When I saw Billy and Frank draw their pistols, I drew my pistol. Billy Clanton leveled his pistol at me, but I did not aim at him. I knew that Frank McLowery had the reputation of being a good shot and a dangerous man and I aimed at him. The first two shots which were fired were fired by Billy Clanton and myself; he shot at me and I shot at Frank McLowery. The fight then became general.*

Three days later, the Territory of Arizona filed murder charges against the Earps and Doc Holliday. The men were fired from their jobs as lawmen and arrested, but they were released from jail on a $10,000 bond. At a hearing in late November, Justice of the Peace Wells Spicer exonerated all of the defendants, saying they were "fully justified in committing these homicides."

THE PLEASANT VALLEY WAR

1887

In the early morning hours of September 4, 1887, Sheriff Commodore Perry Owens walked down the main street of Holbrook, Arizona, intent upon official business. An experienced, Tennessee-born lawman with shoulder-length blond hair and steel-gray eyes, he had reputedly put the rest of the Clanton gang out of business after their shootout with the Earp brothers at the OK Corral in Tombstone. Now, armed with a lever-action Winchester rifle and a Colt .45 pistol, he had come to Holbrook to arrest Andy Cooper.

Cooper's real name was Blevins, and he was wanted in Texas and the Oklahoma Territory for cattle rustling and illicit whiskey dealings with Indians. But these were not the charges that interested the newly elected sheriff of Apache County. Owens had a warrant for Cooper's arrest for stealing horses from the Navajos.

Owens had also heard that Cooper was boasting at the local saloon about killing John Tewksbury and William Jacobs on the Tewksbury ranch several miles south of Holbrook. The sheriff decided to charge Cooper with murder as well.

By the time Owens had reached town, Cooper had gone to the nearby home of a relative to visit his mother; his brother John Blevins, who had participated in the shootout at the Tewksbury ranch; a younger brother, Sam Houston Blevins, who had no criminal record; and several other relatives and friends. Owens went to the house and announced his intent to arrest Andy. When Cooper objected, Owens shot him with his Winchester. John fired at the sheriff but missed and took a shot himself in the shoulder. Owens retreated to the street, only to be followed by Cooper's brother-in-law, Moses Roberts. Owens finished him with a rifle shot to the head. Sam grabbed Andy's gun and was about to fire when Owens stopped him with a shot to the heart.

One of the most famous gunfights in Arizona history had taken less than one minute. And it was only one battle in what would become known as the Pleasant Valley War.

The whole sorry chapter began in 1878, when the Tewksbury family settled in Pleasant Valley along the southern edge of the Mogollon Rim and began breeding horses. Four years later, the Graham family moved into the neighborhood to raise cattle. As the two families got to know each other, the Tewksburys learned that their close neighbors were cattle rustlers, which explained the rapid growth of the Graham herds. When the Tewksburys objected to the Grahams' illegal activities, the entire valley began taking sides.

The feud began in earnest, probably in late 1883, when a neighbor, John Gilliland, and his nephew—both allies of the Grahams—got into a violent argument with Ed Tewksbury. When the smoke cleared, Gilliland and his nephew limped away with gunshot wounds.

In 1884, the Blevins family arrived in the valley and aligned itself with the Grahams. The feud simmered until 1887, when the Tewksburys allowed sheep—anathema to cattle ranchers—to graze on their range. Gunmen hired by the Grahams and Blevinses killed Tewksbury's Basque sheepherder and scared his companions away.

That August, one of the Blevins brothers and some cronies attacked Jim and Ed Tewksbury at nearby Middleton Ranch. After a few minutes of gunfire, Blevins lay dead, and the others escaped with various wounds. Later that month, the brother-in-law of the murdered Basque sheepherder shot and killed eighteen-year-old William Graham.

The feud continued to escalate. Two weeks later, Andy Cooper and John Blevins, with several associates, attacked the Tewksbury ranch house and killed John Tewksbury and William Jacobs. This was the crime that attracted the attention of Sheriff Commodore Perry Owens.

Several more killings occurred in the months and years to come. In 1892, Ed Tewksbury was found guilty of murdering the last of the Graham brothers, Tom, although the evidence clearly showed that a companion, John Rhodes, fired the fatal shot. Ed was imprisoned until 1895, when he was granted a new trial. A year later, his case was dismissed. Ed, the last survivor of the Tewksbury family, died of tuberculosis on April 4, 1904.

The story of the Graham-Tewksbury feud was just too sensational to forget. Several years after the fracas finally ended, Zane Grey revived it in his novel *To the Last Man*.

THE VALOR OF
THE BUFFALO SOLDIERS

1889

Several disheveled men nervously lay in the sand outside Cedar Springs, Arizona Territory, on that hot morning of May 11, 1889. They wiped the sweat from their faces as the sun climbed higher in the cloudless sky. Suddenly, one of the men pointed at a rapidly approaching cloud of dust. He and his companions steeled themselves as a military patrol approached the springs where they were hiding.

The soldiers—members of the Twenty-fourth Infantry and the Tenth Cavalry—were led by Sergeant Benjamin Brown. They were escorting Paymaster J. W. Wham's wagon, filled with script with which to pay the soldiers stationed at forts in the region.

As the patrol neared the spring, the outlaws emerged, filling the air with pistol and rifle fire. When the brief but fierce fight ended, nine enlisted men lay wounded, including Sergeant Brown, who had been shot once in the stomach and once in each arm, and Corporal Isaiah Mays, who, after the soldiers finally beat off the attack, walked and crawled two miles to a ranch house for help.

For their distinguished performance at Cedar Springs, Brown and Mays were awarded the Medal of Honor, the nation's highest military tribute.

Brown and Mays were "buffalo soldiers," as members of the Ninth, Tenth, Twenty-fourth, and Twenty-fifth regiments became known. Authorized in 1866, the four regiments were made up of black soldiers, many of them former slaves (officers, however, were white). For twenty-five years, they saw some of the bloodiest and most vicious fighting west of the Mississippi River. They were one of the most effective weapons in the U.S. arsenal during the Southwestern Indian wars of the 1870s and 1880s.

The buffalo soldiers saw much of their action against the Apaches, but they also were involved in skirmishes with the Ute, Comanche, Cheyenne, Kiowa, and Sioux. The Indians called the black troopers buffalo soldiers either because they had the same respect for the soldiers that they had for the buffalo or because the soldiers' hair reminded them of the thick mane that covered the buffalo's shoulders. The men of the four regiments considered the moniker a compliment.

On more than one occasion, the black regiments came to the rescue of their white counterparts. When the Ninth Cavalry relieved besieged soldiers at the Battle of Milk Creek near the Ute Agency in Colorado in 1879, someone noted that "the gallant dash made by these colored troopers brought them into high favor with the rest of the command, and nothing was considered too good for the 'Buffalo' soldiers after that."

Colonel Benjamin Henry Grierson, the white commander of the Tenth Cavalry, summed up the attitude that most career army officers had toward the buffalo soldiers.

The officers and enlisted men have cheerfully endured many hardships and privations, and in the midst of great dangers steadfastly maintained a most gallant and zealous devotion to duty. . . . They may well be proud of the record made, and rest assured that the hard work undergone in the accomplishment of such . . . valuable service to their country cannot fail, sooner or later, to meet with due recognition and reward.

In addition to their assignments in the American West, the buffalo soldiers went on to fight in the Spanish-American War, where they joined Theodore Roosevelt in his famous charge up San Juan Hill. They served in the Philippines, and in 1916 they rode with one of their old officers, General John Pershing, into Mexico in pursuit of Pancho Villa. Pershing's nickname, Black Jack, was a result of his former duty with the Tenth Cavalry. Finally, during the Korean conflict, the buffalo soldiers' units were integrated into the rest of the army.

THE REMARKABLE CAREER OF PETE KITCHEN

1895

Pete Kitchen was born in Tennessee in 1823—or was it Kentucky in 1822? Authorities disagree. One fact remains certain: Old Pete became a genuine folk hero in his adopted home state of Arizona.

When Kitchen was twenty-four years old, he joined the army and served along the Rio Grande. Eventually, he was transferred to Oregon. After his discharge, he moved to California to try his luck among the recently discovered gold diggings.

In 1853, Kitchen wandered down to Arizona and started a ranch in the Santa Cruz Valley near Tucson, an area that was frequented by bands of hostile Apache Indians. He called his spread "El Potrero"— Spanish for "pastureland"—and, according to his biographer, Gil Procter, in *The Trails of Pete Kitchen,* his 160-acre spread was "the only safe place in the hundred miles between Tucson and Magdalena, Sonora—the bloody road later known as Pete Kitchen's Road."

Kitchen immediately began working on improvements to his ranch. He built a one-room adobe hut, reported to be the first ranch house built by a white settler in Arizona. He hired thirty friendly Indians from nearby Sonora to do the ranching and farming. He also hired two Mexican foremen, and one of them brought along his sister, a dark-eyed beauty who soon became Mrs. Kitchen.

The sudden increase in the ranch's population forced Kitchen to start work on a larger structure. He constructed "The Stronghold" using adobe bricks and stone quarried locally by the Indians. It was a large, fortlike structure with a flat roof and parapets from behind which Kitchen's men could hold off Apache attackers. Additional outbuildings were constructed, and when Kitchen and his bride moved into the Stronghold, he turned over the original one-room adobe to one of his foremen.

By 1859, when Kitchen's wife, Dona Rosa, gave birth to the couple's only child, the ranch was well on its way to self-sufficiency. But the price that Kitchen and his neighbors paid for their independence was awesome. Apache marauders constantly haunted the Arizona-Sonora borderlands, and over the years the residents of El Potrero suffered their share of misery. The little cemetery that Kitchen and his followers had created filled up rapidly as Apache raiders scoured the countryside. Kitchen's greatest loss came in 1871, when his twelve-year-old son, Santiago, was murdered and scalped by members of an Apache war party.

Despite repeated attempts by the Apaches to destroy Kitchen's little community, El Potrero became a haven for travelers who used the long, dangerous road between Tucson and the Mexican villages to the south. Indeed, the ranch was the only haven in the region.

If Kitchen was known for anything other than his hospitality, it was probably for his marksmanship. His reputation for accuracy with pistol and rifle alike soon became legendary throughout southern Arizona and northern Mexico. Years later, a favorite niece who had grown up at El Potrero related the following story about Kitchen's prowess with a rifle.

One day my Uncle Pedro [Pete] saw an Apache up by the rock on the hill across from the house. He always kept a rifle just inside the door for emergencies, and there were rifles in every corner of every room of the house. My uncle knew just where to aim at the rock, because he often shot at it for target practice, and he never missed. He was standing just outside the door at the time, and the door was open. All of a sudden the Indian saw my uncle in the doorway, and jumping up on the rock and turning his back toward Uncle Pedro, he bent over and flipped up his breechclout [sic]. By this time my uncle had picked up his rifle, and when the Indian bent over he killed him right where he used to sit. God rest his soul.

Despite the hardships imposed by the Apaches, Kitchen's ranch prospered. When he finally sold it, he moved to Tucson, where he died August 5, 1895, at the age of seventy-seven. The *Arizona Daily Citizen* carried the news of his death.

The funeral was one of the largest ever seen in this city, for Pete Kitchen's name has long been a household word in Southern Arizona. And so closes the earthly

*career of one of the most remarkable men that ever
faced the frontier dangers of the far Southwest. . . .
Keenly alert to his surroundings, a quick and ready
shot, he bore nothing else than a charmed life and died
in peace, and full of years, surrounded by the comforts
of civilization and friends.*

Today, El Potrero is located about four miles north of Nogales on U.S. Highway 89. Visitors to the restored Stronghold can get some idea of the life of an early Arizona rancher and trader in the days when danger lurked around every corner.

THE LAST BATTLE
OF BUCKEY O'NEILL

1898

It was a bright day in early July 1898, and the nation was preparing to celebrate Independence Day, when Pauline O'Neill stepped out of the train at Prescott, Arizona Territory. Her feet had hardly touched the platform when a telegraph messenger approached and handed her a telegram. As she skimmed the words, her face contorted in pain. The news was devastating. Her beloved husband, William O. ("Buckey") O'Neill, mayor of Prescott, had been killed by Spanish forces in Cuba on July 1.

"The agony was so great that I could not weep for days," she reported later.

The citizens of Prescott were so grief-stricken that they commissioned the world-famous artist Solon Hannibal Borglum to sculpt a statue of O'Neill to be placed on the lawn of the Yavapai County Courthouse.

Who was this Buckey O'Neill? He had been born in 1860 at St. Louis, the first son of Irish parents, John and Mary McMenimin

O'Neill. After the Civil War, in which the elder O'Neill served as a captain in the 116th Pennsylvania Volunteers, the family gravitated to Washington, D.C., where John spent the remainder of his career working as a clerk with the U.S. Treasury Department.

Although there is no proof that Buckey was qualified to practice law, he claimed in an 1879 letter to the secretary of Arizona Territory that he was "a young lawyer, also a practical printer . . . desirous to reap whatever advantage that may accrue by taking the advice of Horace Greeley and seeking a new home and better fortune in the land of the setting sun."

When authorities in Tucson replied favorably to the letter, the nineteen-year-old left Washington and headed for the unknown reaches of Arizona.

O'Neill arrived in Phoenix in September 1879 and quickly got a job as a typesetter at the *Phoenix Herald.* To supplement his income, he also worked part-time as a deputy to the town marshal—a job that required little experience. He earned his nickname, Buckey, because of his willingness to "buck the tiger," or "go for broke" at the local gaming tables.

O'Neill left his job at the *Phoenix Herald* after about six months to become the editor of the newly founded *Arizona Gazette.* Some six months after that, he left Phoenix and moved to Tombstone, where he eventually went to work at the local newspaper, the *Tombstone Epitaph.* Ever-restless, he left Tombstone as suddenly as he had arrived, and by the spring of 1882 he was living in the territorial capital, Prescott, where he established residence for the final sixteen years of his life. He began work for the *Arizona Miner* and later was appointed court reporter for the Third Judicial District Court in Prescott. In 1885, he started his own publication, *Hoof and Horn,* billed as "the only journal devoted exclusively to the Stockgrowing interests of Arizona."

In late 1885, O'Neill fell in love with Pauline Schindler, the twenty-year-old daughter of an army officer stationed at nearby Fort Whipple. The two married in April 1886 and soon found themselves among Prescott's social elite. O'Neill ran for the office of Yavapai County probate judge in 1886 and won by a mere eight votes. The couple's first child died of an illness the following year.

In November 1888, O'Neill was elected sheriff of Yavapai County. His efforts at enforcing the law drew high marks, particularly from an admiring local judge who noted that

> *in an incredibly short time . . . Yavapai County's young*
> *sheriff . . . is in the saddle; and now commences that*
> *pursuit which . . . has scarcely a parallel for daring*
> *and pertinacity in this or any other country. Across vast*
> *sandy plains, up and over rugged mesas and mountains,*
> *through canons and mountain gorges . . . the pursuit*
> *is waged; till at last the robbers are overtaken—a fight*
> *ensues . . . and the robbers are all captured.*

As the candidate of the Populist Party, O'Neill lost a bid for a congressional seat in 1894 and again in 1896. In 1897, he successfully ran for mayor of Prescott. Later that same year, he and his wife adopted a young boy.

O'Neill had been mayor for less than a year when the town received news of the Spanish attack on the U.S. battleship *Maine* while it was at anchor in Havana Harbor, Cuba. Pauline later wrote of her husband's reaction to the news of imminent war with Spain.

> *When the* Maine *was blown up and the whole nation*
> *was discussing the question of the war that might*

follow, Mr. O'Neill felt that his country would
demand his services. A meeting was held . . . in the
courthouse on the evening following the receipt of the
news. Mr. O'Neill again declared that he was ready
and willing to shed his heart's last drop of blood for
his flag, his country.

The United States declared war on Spain on April 25, 1898, and shortly afterwards the governor of the Arizona Territory received a message from the secretary of war.

The President directs that Capt. Leonard Wood of the
U.S. Army be authorized to raise a regiment of cow-
boys and mounted riflemen, and to be its Colonel, and
has named Hon. Theodore Roosevelt as Lt. Colonel.
All other officers will come from the vicinity where the
troops are raised. What can you do for them?

Two days later, O'Neill was appointed a captain in the rapidly formed Arizona contingent that became part of the famous Rough Riders. After a brief training period in Texas and an additional delay in Florida, O'Neill and his companions finally arrived in Cuba on June 22. Nine days later, Mayor Buckey O'Neill was killed when a Spanish bullet tore through his head.

O'Neill was a legend in his own time. Theodore Roosevelt later wrote of him:

A staunchly loyal and generous friend, he was also
exceedingly ambitious on his own account. If, by

risking his life, no matter how great the risk, he could
gain high military distinction, he was bent on gaining
it. He had taken so many chances when death lay on
the hazard, that he felt the odds were now against him.

O'Neill was buried on the hillside where he was killed, but the following year his body was exhumed and reburied in Arlington National Cemetery outside Washington, D.C. In 1891, eight years before his death, he had written an article for a San Francisco newspaper, in which he said that

Death was the black horse that came every day into
every man's camp, and no matter when that day came
a brave man should be booted and spurred and ready
to ride him out.

O'Neill mounted his black horse on that fateful first day of July 1898. True to his own philosophy, he rode it into the pages of history.

THE LAST STAGECOACH ROBBERY

1899

Had it not been potentially dangerous, the last stagecoach robbery in the United States might have been a laughable affair. The unusual pair of robbers were obviously amateurs, and their bungled attempt to get rich quickly not only earned them a place in the history books, but led them straight to jail.

The robbery took place on May 30, 1899, as a salesman, an Eastern visitor, and a Chinese gentleman jounced down the rugged coach road that linked the towns of Benson and Globe. By this time, stagecoaches were almost extinct as a mode of transportation in the United States. One could now travel so much faster and more comfortably by railroad. Nevertheless, a few stages still ran in the more remote areas of the Arizona Territory, and the Benson-Globe express was one of them.

Opinions differ as to whose brainchild the robbery was. Some say it was initiated by Joe Boot, a washed-out, down-on-his-luck miner. Others say it was dreamed up by his partner—a diminutive woman named Pearl Hart who reportedly needed money to send to her ailing mother. In any event, twenty-eight-year-old Hart, armed with a .44 caliber Colt, and Boot, carrying a .45, hid out at a watering spot along the stagecoach route and awaited their prey.

Hart had been raised by respectable parents in Ontario. When she was seventeen, she eloped with Frederick Hart to Chicago, where they worked at the 1893 Colombian Exposition. It might have been among the Wild West shows at the exposition that Pearl decided to leave her husband and try her fortunes in Colorado. Soon after her arrival there, she gave birth to a son. But she was not one to let motherhood slow her down. Pearl simply returned to her parents' home in Ontario and left her son with them. Unfettered, she journeyed to Phoenix.

Life in the Wild West was not exactly what Pearl had expected it to be. To make ends meet, she became a laundress and cook. When her husband, Frederick, showed up one day in 1895, he convinced her to rejoin him, and apparently the couple happily spent the next two or three years together. They had a second child, but domestic life did not suit Frederick, and in 1898 he deserted Pearl, joined the Rough Riders, and rode off to war, apparently never to be heard from again.

Pearl traveled again to her parents' home to present them with their new granddaughter. Alone, she returned to Arizona, where she eventually met Joe Boot. In early 1899, the pair decided to rob the Benson-Globe stage.

Dressed as a man in jeans, boots, and a wide-brimmed hat and waving a pistol, Pearl boldly stepped in front of the oncoming stage, forced the driver to stop, and demanded that he step down. He did, and Pearl disarmed him. In the meantime, Boot had ordered the three passengers out of the coach. While Pearl kept the foursome covered, he took their money—$5 from the Chinese man, $390 from the salesman, and $36 from the Easterner. After sending the stagecoach on its way, Hart and Boot disappeared into the countryside.

Unfortunately, the pair had not planned their escape sufficiently. For three days, they rode aimlessly through the desert wilderness of the Superstition Mountains, completely lost. On the third night, while asleep at a campfire they had made to counter the spring chill, they were discovered by Sheriff William Truman and a small posse and taken to nearby Florence. A mob of curious townspeople gathered, anxious to get a glimpse of the daring robbers. They must have been surprised to see little Hart. In an existing photograph, judging from the rifle she carries, she appears to have been about five feet tall and no more than one hundred pounds.

Jurors at Hart's first trial acquitted her, but the presiding judge was so furious at this travesty of justice that he impaneled a new jury. It found her guilty within ten minutes. She was sentenced to five years in prison at Yuma, while Boot got thirty years.

Hart was released after serving only eighteen months of her sentence, reportedly because the Territorial Prison had not been designed to house female prisoners, and there was no facility in the territory that could. The fact that she had "found religion" may also have played a part. In any event, she walked out of prison a free woman on December 19, 1902.

Moving on to Kansas City, Hart starred in a play her sister had written about her called *The Arizona Bandit*. But the play was a flop, and she reverted to her old ways. She was arrested and briefly jailed in Kansas City for purchasing canned goods she knew to be stolen.

Little is known of Hart's later life. In 1924, she made a nostalgic trip to Arizona and visited the courtroom in which she had been convicted. Some reports say the "Lady Bandit," who made a name for herself by taking part in the last stagecoach robbery in the United States, survived until the mid-1950s.

THE INGLORIOUS DEATH
OF GERONIMO

1909

The Apache war in Arizona and New Mexico had raged for years. The officer in command of the Department of Arizona, General George Crook, had experienced intermittent success with his policy of treating the Apaches as human beings. But always, it seemed, just as progress was being made, something went wrong to send the Indians on the warpath.

Crook thought he had settled the Apache problem once and for all in late March 1886, when he struck an agreement with the primary leader of the Indian resistance, Geronimo. With solemn words and a handshake, the renegade Apache had told Crook:

> *I have little to say. I surrender myself to you. We are all comrades, all one family, all one band. What others say I say also. I give myself up to you. Do with me what you please. I surrender. Once I moved about like the wind. Now I surrender to you and that is all.*

Geronimo had been a leader of the Apache resistance since 1850, when he returned to camp one day to find his mother, wife, and three children murdered by Mexicans. In time, his hatred of Mexicans extended to whites. It was compounded in 1861, when the army tried to capture the Apache leader Cochise while he attended what was supposed to be a friendly meeting near Apache Pass in southeastern Arizona.

Geronimo was a formidable foe. A mastermind at guerrilla warfare, he and a handful of followers kept the army at bay for years. Physically, according to a contemporary account,

> *he was a compactly built, dark-faced man of one hundred and seventy pounds, and about five feet, eight inches in height. The man who once saw his face will never forget it. Crueller features were never cut. The nose was broad and heavy, the forehead low and wrinkled, the chin full and strong, the eyes like two bits of obsidian with a light behind them. The mouth was a most noticeable feature—a sharp, straight, thin-lipped gash of generous length and without one softening curve.*

Unfortunately, after Geronimo's conciliatory meeting with Crook, an unscrupulous white trader sold whiskey to Geronimo's little band, the Indians got drunk, and all of the hard-earned peace negotiations turned out to be for naught. The Apaches returned to their mountain stronghold.

Army authorities in Washington, D.C., quickly tired of Crook's benign policy toward the Apaches. General Philip Sheridan, the Army's commander-in-chief, made it clear to Crook that he wanted the Apache situation resolved.

On April 1, Crook asked to be relieved of his command. He was replaced by General Nelson A. Miles, whose philosophy on the treatment of Indians was entirely different. As summer drew to a close, Miles prepared to capture and force the surrender of Geronimo and his followers. On August 28, 1886, he made clear his thoughts on the disposition of the subdued Apaches in a telegram to the acting secretary of war.

> *My purpose was . . . to move them [the Apaches] at least 1,200 miles east, completely disarm them, send their stock, for the winter at least, to Fort Union, N. Mex., scatter the grown children through the identical schools of the country, and hold the balance at one or two military posts, where they would acquire the habits of industry, until such time as the Government should provide them permanent residence and means of self-support. By this means they would be completely under control, they would be satisfied, and the people relieved of their presence without loss of life. Geronimo has been notified that he can surrender, but subject to the disposition of the Government.*

On September 3, Miles and Geronimo met at a place called Skeleton Canyon, and Geronimo and his tiny group turned themselves over to the army.

The circumstances surrounding Geronimo's surrender to Miles have been debated for years. The captured Apaches were under the impression that they would immediately be reunited with their families in Florida, where a large number of previously captured Apaches had already been sent. Instead, the army scattered the Indians, some of them ending up in prison at Fort Marion in St. Augustine, Florida, and some at Fort Pickens in Pensacola Bay. Geronimo did not see his second family for two years.

In 1894, Geronimo and the rest of the Apaches imprisoned in Florida were sent to Fort Sill, in today's Oklahoma. By then, scores had already died in the humid, disease-ridden cells of their Florida prisons. Many more died in Oklahoma before the remainder were allowed to return to their Arizona homeland.

Geronimo was never to see his home again. U.S. officials trotted him around the nation, allowing curious tourists to peer at him and purchase his photograph for twenty-five cents. He appeared at the Louisiana Purchase Exposition in St. Louis in 1904 and rode in President Theodore Roosevelt's inaugural parade in 1905. In 1908, the frustrated Apache told a newspaper reporter:

> *I want to go back to my old home before I die. Tired of fight and want to rest. Want to go back to the mountains again. I asked the Great White Father to allow me to go back, but he said no.*

On February 17, 1909, Geronimo, the last great war chief of the Apache Indians, died at Fort Sill at the age of eighty-six. If military strategy still meant anything to him on his deathbed, he may have recalled with satisfaction that, before he surrendered to General Miles, he and his two-score followers had for years eluded five thousand of America's best troopers.

THE LONG ROAD TO STATEHOOD

1912

On St. Valentine's Day 1912, at exactly 8:55 in the morning, the telegraph station in Phoenix received a message from President William Howard Taft to Territorial Governor Richard E. Sloan. As he took the wire from the delivery boy, Sloan must have guessed what the message would say. He ripped open the envelope and smiled broadly as he read. "Gentlemen, Arizona is now a state," he declared to his aides.

And so Arizona became the forty-eighth state of the Union, the last of the contiguous United States.

The road to statehood had been a long and arduous one for the people of the Arizona Territory. Since 1889, when the Fifteenth Territorial Legislature had called for a constitutional convention, Arizonans had been actively advocating statehood. Earlier, in 1846, when General Stephen Watts Kearny and his Army of the West had occupied Santa Fe without firing a shot, Arizona had been recognized as part of New Mexico. Arizonans had dreamed of having their own government ever since. Their dream seemed within reach in 1863, when President Abraham Lincoln split the New Mexico Territory in two and created a separate Territory of Arizona.

From 1863 to 1889, Arizonans were content with their territorial status. But the desire for statehood grew. When the 1889 call for a constitutional convention was quashed by the governor, the Sixteenth Legislature issued a new call in 1891. This time, delegates were elected, and the convention assembled in Phoenix, the new capital, in September. The proposed constitution was adopted by Arizona voters in December.

In 1892, Arizona's delegate to the U.S. House of Representatives, Marcus A. Smith, proposed legislation to grant Arizona statehood. The bill passed the House but failed in the Senate. An identical bill passed the House in 1893 but again failed to get by the Senate.

Despite the lack of encouragement from Washington, D.C., Arizonans continued to prepare for statehood. In 1897, the territorial assembly voted to build a capitol in Phoenix, and four years later the structure was completed and occupied. In 1902, Congressman Smith reintroduced his statehood bill. Again, it passed the House but failed even to generate action in the Senate.

In May 1902, Congress considered legislation to admit Arizona and New Mexico to the Union as a single state called Montezuma. The House approved the bill two years later, but the following year the Arizona Territorial Legislature advised Congress that it was not in favor of such a move. In 1906, Congress decided to let citizens of both territories vote on the issue. Arizonans voted five to one against the measure, while New Mexicans voted two to one in favor. Since both territories did not approve the referendum, the single-statehood bill failed.

In 1908, President Theodore Roosevelt urged Congress to consider separate statehood for Arizona and New Mexico. In January

1910, the Arizona statehood bill passed the House; five months later, it passed the Senate. For the rest of that year, delegates to a new constitutional convention hammered out a state constitution. Voters approved it by a margin of three to one.

Then, in August 1911, President William Howard Taft vetoed the Arizona statehood bill because of a measure in the state constitution that would allow voters to recall, or remove from office, elected judges. In his veto message, Taft wrote:

> *This provision of the Arizona constitution, in its application to county and State judges, seems to me so pernicious in its effect, so destructive of independence in the judiciary, so likely to subject the rights of the individual to the possible tyranny of a popular majority, and therefore, to be so injurious to the cause of free government, that I must disapprove a constitution containing it. . . . By the recall in the Arizona constitution it is proposed to give to the majority power to remove arbitrarily, and without delay, any judge who may have the courage to render an unpopular decision. . . . We can not be blind to the fact that often an intelligent and respectable electorate may be so roused upon an issue that it will visit with condemnation the decision of a just judge, though exactly in accord with the law governing the case, merely because it affects unfavorably their contest.*

Taft agreed to grant Arizona statehood *if* voters there would remove judicial recall from the constitution. In December, they did just that, and on the following February 14, the president signed the proclamation that admitted Arizona into the brother-hood of states.

In Phoenix that same day, W. P. Hunt took the oath of office as the first governor of the state of Arizona. Ironically, nine months later, voters approved a measure that would restore judicial recall to the state constitution.

FRANK LUKE'S FINAL FLIGHT

1918

Frank Luke was just four months past his twentieth birthday when he left his parents' comfortable home in Phoenix to enlist in the Aviation Section of the U.S. Signal Corps. He had talked to his sister, Eva, a Red Cross nurse stationed in Europe, about whether he should join the service. Much to his surprise, she had thought it was a good idea. And so, on September 25, 1917, Luke joined the Army and began a hectic, adventurous—but short—career that would make his name a household word in Arizona.

Luke was commissioned a second lieutenant on January 3, 1918, and by March he was stationed in France. After additional flight and gunnery training, he was assigned to the Twenty-seventh Aero Squadron of the First Pursuit Group. The airplanes that made up the Twenty-seventh were Spad 13s; each was equipped with a 220-horsepower engine and two Vickers machine guns. Maximum speed was 139 miles an hour, and maximum combat range was 185 miles.

By mid-August, Luke was flying combat missions. He shot down his first German plane while he was escorting a U.S. camera plane that was taking photographs of the German lines. When he returned to base, Luke boasted that he "never pulled the triggers until I had my gun right in that baby's cockpit. And I didn't leave him until he hit the ground and rolled over on his back, with me not more than 200 feet in the air."

At about this same time, Luke discovered German observation balloons suspended high above the ground. These highly flammable balloons were manned by soldiers whose job it was to scout the surrounding countryside for enemy troop movements. Usually they were protected by antiaircraft and machine guns, and sometimes, from above, by German aircraft.

The danger did not faze happy-go-lucky Luke, who viewed life as a game that would be won by the best man. And Luke knew he was the best!

Luke spent six weeks on the front lines, accumulating thirty air hours in seventeen combat missions. During that time, he destroyed at least fifteen enemy observation balloons and four German planes.

On September 29, Luke climbed into his Spad, taxied down the runway, and flew off into the dusk. This would be his last flight. His mission was to destroy three German observation balloons that had recently been spotted in the neighborhood of Verdun, France. Within minutes he sighted and shot down the first balloon. His Spad was hit by gunfire, but he managed to escape the eight German fighter planes that trailed him for a few miles.

Luke destroyed the second balloon and then the third. As he fired his machine guns at his final target, it suddenly exploded, possibly sending flames high enough to engulf Luke's low-flying aircraft. In any event, the plane was severely damaged, and Luke had to crash-land in a nearby field.

Luke was cleaning his wounds in a creek when he was surrounded by several German soldiers, who demanded his surrender.

Brave to the end, he drew his pistol and fired into the German ranks until he, himself, was killed. Residents of Verdun recovered his body and buried it nearby.

Luke's last day of glory won him the Medal of Honor, the highest honor that can be bestowed upon a soldier. He is one of only twenty-one Arizona heroes to receive the coveted award. His citation reads in part:

> *After having previously destroyed a number of enemy aircraft within 17 days he voluntarily started on a patrol after German observation balloons. Though pursued by 8 German planes which were protecting the enemy balloon line, he unhesitatingly attacked and shot down in flames 3 German balloons, being himself under heavy fire from ground batteries and the hostile planes. . . . Forced to make a landing and surrounded on all sides by the enemy, who called upon him to surrender, he drew his automatic pistol and defended himself gallantly until he fell dead from a wound in the chest.*

THE TREE-RING SECRET

1929

It was a hot, dry afternoon in the rolling desert of what would one day be northeastern Arizona. The year was about A.D. 1200, and the bronzed men who squatted around a large pine log were members of a late Ancestral Puebloan tribe, the forebearers of whom had settled this area hundreds of years previously.

Nearby, several women and older girls were busy preparing the evening meal. The younger children, accompanied by a few yapping dogs, played hide-and-seek among the giant boulders.

The men had just finished stripping the bark from the hefty log. Now they lifted it and carried it across a rock-strewn area to the base of a small cliff. Other men, occupying positions on the edge of the cliff about twenty feet above the ground, dropped crudely woven ropes to their companions below. The men on the ground tied the ropes around both ends of the log and, when all was ready, called to the men above to hoist the heavy object upward. Next, the men on the cliff delivered the log to a party of workers building a single-room dwelling.

The back part of the structure was partially carved out of the rock face of an adjoining cliff, and the front had been enclosed with carefully laid rock walls. The men raised the skinned log to the top of the room and rested it on opposite walls, where it became a beam to support the building's roof.

A little more than seven hundred years later, another man crouched beneath the decaying beams of this same cliff dwelling. He was Andrew Ellicott Douglass, an astronomer at the University of Arizona and director of the Steward Observatory in Tucson. In recent years, Douglass had developed a new science called "dendrochronology," or as it was commonly called, "tree-ring dating." He was searching now for building logs even older than those he had already dated back to A.D. 1260.

The science of dendrochronology hinges upon the fact that the amount of rainfall in a given area determines how close together the annual rings of trees grow. By comparing the distance between the rings of a tree of known age with the rings of an undated specimen, a scientist can determine the age of that specimen and thereby date past events.

The technique revolutionized the science of archaeology. It enabled scientists to precisely date a variety of cultures and their artifacts.

Several years after his arrival in Arizona, Douglass had hit upon the idea of comparing growth rings in recently cut trees with those in ancient timbers. He had come to Flagstaff in 1894 to assist Percival Lowell at his newly built observatory there. Douglass believed that sunspot activity directly influenced the climate on earth, and by 1909, he had found the evidence he needed to prove his theory. During his research, he discovered that a direct correlation existed between rainfall and tree-ring growth.

Over the next few years, Douglass worked closely with archaeologists as he attempted to construct a chronology that would allow timbers in pueblos and cliff dwellings to be dated accurately. When he was unable to go back any farther than about A.D. 1300, he prevailed upon the Hopi Indians of northern Arizona to allow him to bore into the log beams of their pueblos and obtain samples of the wood for his experiments. But even those ancient timbers did not go back far enough to bridge the gap between 1300 and some much older timbers he had found in several ancient cliff ruins.

It was the samples that Douglass took from the deserted cliff dwelling in northeastern Arizona in 1929 that did the trick. Sponsored by the National Geographic Society, Douglass's latest research allowed him to bridge the gap. The wood from the burned beam at the cliff ruin pushed his timeline back to A.D. 700, and over the next five years, Douglass extended it even further, to A.D. 11.

The practical application of dendrochronology extends far beyond helping archaeologists to date their findings. Tree-ring dating has now proven that during the early part of the twentieth century, when the federal government was studying the allocation of water resources in the Colorado River basin, rainfall was more plentiful than it had been in the past four hundred years. Therefore, the allocation of valuable water to the various states was based on atypical and misleading data. The result was that the Colorado River was vastly over-allocated, and when rainfall returned to normal, the river and its valley suffered accordingly.

Douglass founded the Laboratory of Tree-Ring Research at the University of Arizona in 1937 and served as its director until 1958. Under his leadership, the laboratory became the world's largest and best center for the new science of dendrochronology. Douglass died in Tucson in 1962.

THE DISCOVERY OF PLUTO

1930

Night after night during the winter of 1929–30, young Clyde W. Tombaugh, an astronomy assistant at the Lowell Observatory in Flagstaff, recorded the light received through the observatory's giant telescope on sensitive photographic plates. During the day, Tombaugh carefully compared each photograph with those taken on previous nights. If a point of light appeared in a different position on a plate than it had previously, this would be an indication that Tombaugh might have discovered a new planet.

Astronomers had been searching for a ninth planet in the solar system for a long time. In 1894, Percival Lowell, a wealthy Boston astronomer, had used his own money to build Lowell Observatory high on a mountain peak outside Flagstaff. The clear, dry air provided a perfect atmosphere through which to observe the heavens, and soon after Lowell arrived in Arizona he began his search for "Planet X."

Through a complex set of mathematical equations that took into account among other things the orbit and rotation of the planet Uranus, Lowell had concluded that yet another planet circled the sun. For years, Lowell and his associates methodically and laboriously hunted for the elusive Planet X, but by 1916, when he died of a stroke, he still had not found it.

To help them with the tedious work of reviewing the millions of stars that appeared in the photographs taken each night, observatory officials hired young Tombaugh, an amateur astronomer from Kansas. They probably would have smiled and passed off as fantasy Tombaugh's "last will" in his high school yearbook. It predicted that "Comet Clyde," as he was called, would "discover a new world."

And so he did, at four o'clock on the afternoon of February 18, 1930. Comparing photographic plates exactly as he had done so many times before, Tombaugh suddenly noticed evidence of a definite movement. Going over the plates again and again to assure himself, young Tombaugh at last decided that he had, indeed, discovered Lowell's Planet X. He could hardly contain his excitement as he reported his find to the observatory's director, Vesto Melvin Slipher. Night after night of additional photography and comparison of plates proved beyond a shadow of a doubt that the Kansas amateur's claim was valid.

The astronomers decided to delay announcing the discovery until March 13, which not only had been Lowell's birthday, but was the anniversary of Frederick William Herschel's discovery in 1781 of Uranus. The March 24, 1930, issue of *Time* magazine relayed the news to the American public.

The inhabitants of Earth learned last week that there is another planet, beside the eight they knew about, revolving around the Sun as the earth does. A few of Earth's inhabitants had known the news for some time. The late Percival Lowell (1855–1916), rich traveler

turned astronomer, elder brother of President Abbott
Lawrence Lowell of Harvard University and of the
late poetess Amy Lowell (1874–1925), in 1915 had
predicted the existence of another member of the Planet
System on its outer fringe.

For some time after the planet's discovery, the nagging question of what to name it took the limelight. Mrs. Lowell, Percival's widow, suggested "Percival." Other suggestions included Isis, Lilith, Vulcan, and Minerva. What astronomical symbol to assign to the planet was just as troublesome. Finally, Slipher, the observatory director, received a telegram from the professor of astronomy at Oxford University, noting that a young English girl, Venetia Burney, had suggested the name "Pluto." And so Pluto it was. Its astronomical sign became "PL," the first two letters of the new name, as well as Percival Lowell's initials.

The public was flabbergasted by the sheer size of the solar system, enlarged as it was by the discovery of Pluto. *Time* attempted to describe its proportions in everyday terms.

The immensity of the solar system can be grasped by
considering Augusta, Me., as the sun and Sacramento,
Calif., 2,663 air miles away, as the New Planet. Earth
would then circle through Portland, Me., Mercury
through Wiscasset, Me., Venus through Rockland,
Me., Mars through Bar Harbor, Me., Jupiter through
Bridgeport, Conn., Saturn through Annapolis, Md.,
Uranus through Nashville, Tenn., Neptune through
Oklahoma City.

For three-quarters of a century, Pluto was recognized by astronomers the world over as the ninth planet. During the past few years, however, with the advent of more powerful telescopes, not to mention the placement of observatories on far-reaching spacecraft, it has become necessary to reevaluate Pluto. The former planet has now been found to be only one of nearly seventy thousand similar objects—most smaller, but some, much larger—in the Kuiper Belt which extends in outer space from Neptune's orbit to a distance equal to fifty-five times that between Earth and the Sun. Accordingly, in August 2006, at Prague, Czech Republic, members of the International Astronomical Union demoted Pluto to "dwarf planet" status. In the meantime, NASA has launched a spacecraft that will reach the vicinity of Pluto in 2015 and transmit images back to Earth.

THE INTEGRITY OF
TRADER HUBBELL

1930

Shortly after establishing a trading post among the Navajo Indians in 1878, Lorenzo Hubbell faced a situation that, had it turned out differently, could have nipped in the bud a fifty-two year career as the tribe's most influential and respected trader. Hubbell had moved to Ganado, Arizona Territory, from Fort Wingate, New Mexico Territory, where he had worked as a trader's clerk. Born near Albuquerque in 1853, he was the son of a Connecticut emigrant father and a native New Mexican woman. He spoke fluently both the Navajo language and his mother's native Spanish.

Hubbell's crisis occurred when a local Navajo man came into the new trading post to get flour. Hubbell dipped the requested amount out of a large barrel, dumped it into a cloth sack, and gave it to the man, who promptly turned and walked out the door without paying. Hubbell called to the man several times but got no response. Finally, he jumped over the counter and pursued the Navajo, catching him in the front yard of the trading post. Despite the fact that the Indian was considerably larger than he was, Hubbell grabbed the man by the hair and wrestled him to the ground.

About seventy-five curious Navajos watched in amazement as the bespectacled Hubbell twisted the big Indian's ear and forced him back into the trading post. After the man had returned the sack of flour to the counter, Hubbell went outside and addressed the crowd.

"Come on any of you who think you can steal from me," he challenged. "I'll twist the ears of any Indian who wants to try it."

Nodding silent understanding, the Indians in the crowd quickly dispersed, and from that day until his death in 1930, Hubbell had no further trouble with thievery at his trading post.

Hubbell befriended the Navajos, who called him "Double Glasses" and sometimes "Old Mexican." He was not the first trader in the region. Kit Carson's paralyzing raid on Canyon de Chelly in 1863–64 had completely demoralized the Navajos, and thousands of them had been marched to the Apache reservation in New Mexico Territory. After a few years of misery, the Navajos were allowed to return to their beloved homeland in northern Arizona. Soon, white traders quick to sniff a potential profit established several posts at which to trade with the tribe.

Hubbell's post was one of the finest in all the Navajo Nation. He stocked everything imaginable, including sugar, coffee, flour, canned goods, candy, and tobacco. The women could find calico cloth, beads, yarn, and muslin, while their husbands could buy pocketknives, harnesses, all types of hardware, rope, and ready-made clothes. For these wonderful commodities, the Navajos gladly traded their beautiful handmade wool blankets.

But the post was more than a place for trading and haggling over prices. It was also a social gathering place, where people gossiped and exchanged the latest news from back East. It was the Hubbell family home as well and sheltered Lorenzo, his wife, Lina Rubi, and eventually their two sons and daughter.

Hubbell was an honest man. He frowned on unscrupulous traders who took advantage of Indians for profit. He once wrote:

> *The first job of an Indian trader, in my belief, is to look after the material welfare of his neighbors; to advise them to produce that which their natural inclinations and talent best adapts them; to treat them honestly and insist upon getting the same treatment from them . . . to find a market for their products and vigilantly watch that they keep improving in the production of same, and advise them which commands the best price.*

At one time, the Hubbells operated several other trading posts throughout northern Arizona. During the 1880s, Lorenzo served as sheriff of Apache County, and when Arizona became a state in 1912, he was elected to the first legislature. He was unsuccessful in a bid for a U.S. Senate seat, however.

Hubbell was a guiding force among the Navajo Indians during the late 1800s and early 1900s. When he died in 1930, he left a vacuum that could scarcely be filled. Perhaps the tribute of a Navajo friend best sums up his importance.

> *You wear out your shoes, you buy another pair; When the food is all gone, you buy more; You gather melons, and more will grow on the vine; You grind your corn and make bread which you eat; And next year you*

*have plenty more corn. But my friend Don Lorenzo is
gone, and none to take his place.*

The Hubbell family continued running the trading post at
Ganado after Lorenzo's death. When Roman, the last surviving child,
died in 1957, his wife, Dorothy, decided to sell it. However, because
she did not want to fragment the family's fantastic collection of more
than 200,000 artifacts, she stayed on for eight more years. Finally,
she offered the trading post to the federal government. Through the
efforts of Senator Barry Goldwater and Congressman Stewart Udall,
the property was purchased by the National Park Service and is now
maintained as a national historic site.

THE BIGGEST DAM IN THE WORLD

1936

On a warm Sunday afternoon in early March 1936, two men faced each other in the middle of the roadway that ran across the top of the newly completed Boulder Dam, high above the Colorado River. The men were Frank T. Crowe, of San Francisco's Six Companies, Inc., the engineer in charge of construction of the dam, and Ralph Lowry, of the U.S. Bureau of Reclamation. In a simple ceremony, Crowe firmly grasped Lowry's hand and quietly said, "Take it, it's yours now." With those brief words, the magnificent Boulder Dam, the largest such structure in the world, became the property of the U.S. government.

Boulder Dam had been the dream of many people since the turn of the century. In October 1897, Dr. Elwood Mead—the Wyoming engineer after whom Lake Mead, the reservoir behind Boulder Dam, was named—suggested impounding the waters of the Colorado River for storage. By 1922, Secretary of Commerce Herbert Hoover had represented federal interests in scores of preliminary meetings with delegates from Arizona, California, Colorado, Nevada, New

Mexico, Utah, and Wyoming to discuss allocation of water from the Colorado River to those states.

In December 1928, Congress authorized construction of a dam on the Colorado River by passing legislation known as the Boulder Canyon Project Act. The proposed site for the dam was in Boulder Canyon, sometimes called Black Canyon.

Time magazine reported on the monster project in its February 10, 1930, issue.

> *Boulder Canyon is a great gorge on the deep-sunk Colorado River between Arizona and Nevada. Between its rock walls the U.S. is to build the world's largest dam, 700 ft. high, less than 1,000 ft. wide. Behind the dam's arch will form a deep narrow lake, 100 miles long, voluminous enough to flood the state of Kentucky under a foot of water. The development has three purposes: 1) Flood control for the lower Colorado; 2) Irrigation for barren lands in Arizona and Nevada; 3) Electric current from the 600,000 h.p. of falling water. Total cost: $165,000,000.*

The final construction site was selected by A. P. Davis, the director of the U.S. Bureau of Reclamation, and approved by a panel of expert geologists, hydrologists, and engineers. On July 3, 1930, President Herbert Hoover signed the document that formally initiated construction. Six Companies, Inc., of San Francisco was the low bidder. By contract, the company had 2,565 days to finish the project. The target date was April 11, 1938. As it turned out, the contractor finished the work with more than twenty-five months to spare.

In late September 1935, President Hoover's successor, Franklin D. Roosevelt, visited the nearly completed Boulder Dam and formally dedicated it to the American people.

> *This great Boulder Dam warrants universal approval because it will prevent floods and flood damage, because it will irrigate thousands of acres of tillable land and because it will generate electricity to run the wheels of many factories and illuminate countless homes.*

Taking the opportunity to promote some of his own public works projects as well, he added:

> *These great Government power projects will affect not only the development of agriculture and industry and mining in the sections they serve, but they will also prove useful yardsticks to measure the cost of power throughout the United States. It is my belief that the Government should proceed to lay down the first yardstick.*

Although the dam was originally named for President Hoover, it gradually became known as Boulder Dam after the president left office. However, in 1947, President Harry S. Truman signed a resolution restoring the original name, Hoover Dam, to the structure. It is known by that name today.

The statistics of Hoover Dam are awesome. Standing 726.4 feet high, 1,282 feet long, 660 feet thick at its base, and 45 feet thick at the crest, the dam was made with 3.25 million cubic feet of concrete. The two spillways at the dam's base are capable of passing 400,000 feet of water every second. The building that houses the power plant is 1,650 feet long, and the plant itself is designed to have a maximum output of 1.8 million horsepower. Hoover Dam's reservoir, Lake Mead, backs upriver for 115 miles and has a shoreline of 550 miles. Its storage capacity is nearly 33 million acre-feet.

Although they have since been surpassed in size, Hoover Dam was the largest dam in the world when it was completed in 1936, and Lake Mead was the largest man-made lake.

ZANE GREY'S LOVE AFFAIR
WITH ARIZONA

1939

When Zane Grey died in 1939, he was one of the most popular writers in America. His eighty-five books and numerous short stories provided inspiration for more than one hundred movies starring such Hollywood luminaries as John Wayne, Randolph Scott, Maureen O'Sullivan, and Wallace Beery. By the mid-1970s, Grey's books had sold in excess of forty million copies and had been translated into twenty foreign languages. Only Louis L'Amour and Frederick Faust (who wrote under a number of pseudonyms, the most popular of which was Max Brand) have matched Grey's prodigious output of western fiction.

Twenty-five of Grey's novels were set in Arizona. He first visited the area in 1907, at the invitation of Charles Jesse ("Buffalo") Jones, a noted hunter who had lately devoted his life to the preservation of the American bison. Thirty-five years old at the time, Grey traveled West with the awe and fascination of a child. His life was changed forever.

To Grey, Arizona was like no place else on earth. He learned to shoot, rope, ride horseback, and camp in the rugged mountains and vast deserts. Until this time, he had set his novels in the Ohio River valley. But Arizona changed all that. From then on, the American West would provide the backdrop for most of Grey's novels.

The beauty of the Arizona Territory overwhelmed Grey from the very beginning. Of the Painted Desert, he wrote:

> *Imagination had pictured the desert for me as a vast, sandy plain, flat and monotonous. Reality showed me desolate mountains gleaming bare in the sun, long lines of red bluffs, white sand dunes, and hills of blue clay, areas of level ground—in all, a many-hued, boundless world in itself, wonderful and beautiful, fading all around into the purple haze of deceiving distance. . . . How infinite all this is! How impossible to understand!*

The majesty of the Grand Canyon was also beyond his "Eastern" comprehension. He wrote:

> *This cataclysm of the earth, this playground of a river was not inscrutable; it was only inevitable—as inevitable as nature herself. Millions of years in the bygone ages it had lain serene under a live moon; it would bask silent under a rayless sun, in the onward edge of time. It spoke simply, though its words were grand: "My spirit is the Spirit of Time, of Eternity, of God. Man is little, vain, vaunting. Listen. Tomorrow he shall be gone."*

Grey was born on January 31, 1872, in Zanesville, Ohio, a town named for his ancestors. As a child, he loved baseball and in fact was such an outstanding player that he was offered a baseball scholarship at the University of Pennsylvania, from which he graduated in 1896. He moved to New York and opened a dental office on West 74th Street, where he practiced for several years.

In 1903, Grey published his first book, *Betty Zane,* a tale of the Ohio River valley during the American Revolution. Many of his characters had been inspired by his own ancestors, and the book met with moderate success. It also changed Grey's life. He deserted his dentistry practice and vowed to devote the remainder of his life to writing. *Betty Zane* was followed by two more volumes of what became a trilogy, *Spirit of the Border* and *The Last Trail.*

From that point on, writing became an obsession with Grey. After his Arizona sojourn with "Buffalo" Jones, he churned out *The Last of the Plainsmen.* It was quickly followed by several other books with Arizona settings.

Grey's work coincided with a time in American history when a glorified image of the Old West was extremely popular. Readers wanted two-fisted action and blood and guts in their books. Grey gave it to them. But more importantly, Grey also gave his readers a *genuine* glimpse of the West in those days when it was being "tamed." He prided himself on his historical accuracy to the point where his books provided not only action and adventure, but American history lessons as well.

In 1918, Grey moved to California, where he continued to provide his rapidly growing following with book after book. In 1925, he published the title for which he most wanted to be remembered: *The Vanishing American.* At the risk of offending the Bureau of Indian Affairs, as well as several religious organizations, Grey sympathetically portrayed the plight of the American

Indian. And it took him only a month and a half to write the entire manuscript!

Although Grey's critics have called his literary contributions everything from "primitive" to "sentimentalized escape literature of the most banal kind," the fact remains that his books are still read by a vast American audience. Only recently, his first book, *Betty Zane,* was reissued in paperback by a major American publisher. And the Western Writers of America, an organization of hundreds of professional fiction and nonfiction writers of the American West, voted Grey one of the first members of its "Hall of Fame."

Regardless of how one views his literary accomplishments, Grey is an icon in the literature of the American West. He was one of the first—and one of the most prolific—writers to give the American public what it wanted to read about the glorious days of the Wild West.

THE MAKING OF
BARRY GOLDWATER

1964

As election day approached in 1964, Barry Goldwater was at the peak of his career. He faced incumbent Lyndon Johnson in the race for the presidency of the United States. He had actually wanted to run against John F. Kennedy, but that desire was cut short on that fateful day in November 1963, when Kennedy was assassinated. Goldwater agreed to stay in the race, he said, for the good of the Republican Party.

Goldwater and Kennedy had been steadfast friends. From their early days in the U.S. Senate in the mid-1950s, when both sat on the McClellan Rackets Committee, the two men, despite their broad political differences, liked and respected each other. After Kennedy was elected president in 1960, Goldwater kept a close eye on his friend's administration. After the Bay of Pigs debacle, the Cuban missile crisis, and increased American involvement in Vietnam, Goldwater made up his mind to seek the Republican nomination in 1964.

Goldwater wrote about his decision to challenge Kennedy in his autobiography, *Goldwater,* published in 1988.

> *A Kennedy-Goldwater clash would have been quite different from my campaign against Lyndon Johnson. It would have been a direct and continuing attack on Kennedy policies, with much less time spent on irrelevancies. Kennedy and I formally agreed—it seems a pipe dream in looking at some of today's negative campaigning—that we would ride the same plane or train to several stops and debate face to face on the same platform. I was convinced I would do well because of my deep commitment to the conservative cause. Kennedy was a Democrat by accident of birth; he was more a pragmatist than a Democrat. Kennedy spouted the liberal line but was cynical about much of it. I was a conservative by personal conviction.*

Goldwater had already lived an interesting life by the time he ran for president in 1964. He was born to Josephine and Baron Goldwater in Phoenix in 1909, three years before Arizona became a state. Small farms and ranches dotted the Salt and Verde river valleys, supporting the ten thousand or so residents of Phoenix.

The Goldwater name had been prominent in Arizona since 1860, when Barry's grandfather, Michel ("Big Mike") brought a wagonload full of merchandise from California to Gila City, a small mining town nestled on the Gila River. In 1862, Michel and his younger brother, Joseph, opened a general store in La Paz, Arizona, and in time they became prominent and prosperous merchants. Michel's son Morris joined his father and uncle in 1867, and eighteen years later, Baron Goldwater became a part of the business as well.

Barry Goldwater may have inherited his political aspirations from his Uncle Morris, a two-time mayor of Prescott and the founder of the Arizona Democratic Party. Morris was instrumental in framing the state constitution and was the Grand Master of Arizona Masons. He became like a second father to Barry when Baron died.

Upon his father's death, Barry quit his courses at the University of Arizona and joined the family business. Years later he wrote:

> *That was the biggest mistake of my life. It would have been much better to somehow remain in school and graduate from college. I've long had misgivings about my education being cut short. My career would have been more fulfilling if I'd had additional history, economics, and other courses. Each of us, whether we go into private business or the business of government, needs the most education we can get. Both men and women are disadvantaged—I don't care what their other background may be—if they don't fulfill their intellectual potential.*

Goldwater quickly adapted to the mercantile business, and in 1937 he became president of the firm, which then had fifty-five employees working in stores in Phoenix and Prescott. He also became fascinated with airplanes. From his first solo flight in 1929, through his personal involvement with the formation of the Arizona Air National Guard, to his retirement from the Air Force Reserve as a major general, flying continued to be a significant part of Goldwater's life.

Public service was Goldwater's other love. He served on the Colorado River Commission, the U.S. Department of Interior's Advisory Commission on Indian Affairs, and the Arizona Interstate Stream Commission. In 1949, he entered politics with his election to the Phoenix City Council. Although Arizona was predominantly a Democratic state, Goldwater was elected to the U.S. Senate in 1952, running on the Republican ticket. He would serve as a senator for thirty years.

Goldwater lost the 1964 presidential election to Johnson by a landslide. The final popular vote was 43 million for Johnson to Goldwater's 27 million. Goldwater took the states of Arizona, Alabama, Georgia, Louisiana, Mississippi, and South Carolina. But, despite his defeat, he believed he strengthened the Republican Party. And that, after all, was what he had set out to do. Nearly a quarter of a century after the defeat, Goldwater wrote:

> *Some of us believe the conservative movement has had broader and deeper national implications than any other movement of our times. The reasons are that it now reaches beyond single segments of the population into all classes of society, and it is involved in virtually every major issue facing the nation. Conservatives now hail from all regions of the country, every social class, each and every creed and color, and all age groups. The new GOP was forged in the fires of the 1964 presidential campaign.*

Following his unsuccessful presidential bid, Goldwater sat out the next four years as a private citizen, a time in his life he called "four of the most satisfying years I have had as an adult." He was returned to the Senate in 1968, serving until 1986 when he retired to Arizona. He suffered a debilitating stroke ten years later and died at his home in Paradise Valley on May 29, 1998.

Of all the politicians, statesmen, and public servants who were active in the twentieth century, Goldwater will be remembered as the man who made conservatism in politics "respectable." He, above all others, rekindled the dimmed principles of those individual freedoms that made the United States a great power to begin with.

THE DEMISE OF A HIGHWAY

1984

Williams is a small town of around 3,200 people, snuggled in the Prescott National Forest in northeastern Arizona. Named in honor of the grizzled old mountain man, William Sherley (Old Bill) Williams, who trapped in the surrounding region for beaver and traded with the Indians during the 1820s and '30s, the community lies at the crossroads of Interstate 40 and State Route 64. At an altitude of around 6,800 feet, the town's primary industry today is tourism, annually serving hundreds of thousands of visitors to the South Rim of the Grand Canyon, only one hour's drive away.

On October 13, 1984, several hundred residents of Williams, along with a few neighboring ranchers, gathered in town to pay their respects. The deceased, well-known by all those present, had passed away at the age of only fifty-eight. Born in Chicago in 1926, just before the arrival of the Great Depression, the dearly departed had slowly moved through the states of Illinois, Missouri, Kansas, Oklahoma, Texas, New Mexico, and Arizona, before reaching journey's end at Santa Monica, California in 1937. Now, as the onlookers in

Williams sadly noted, the final, exhausted remains of U.S. Route 66 were laid to rest and a short section of the newly completed I-40 was declared its replacement. With the dedication of the Williams segment of the interstate highway and following nearly six decades of service to American drivers, the old road was officially retired, and no traces of the legendary Route 66 exist either in signage or on road maps.

Route 66, like many highways before it, and no doubt many more to follow, was a victim of the times. The thoroughfare was the brainchild of Cyrus Stevens Avery, a Tulsa, Oklahoma, real estate, coal, and oil magnate, who, in 1924, was a leader in the American Association of State Highway Officials and instrumental in drafting a document to U.S. Secretary of Agriculture Howard M. Gore anticipating the Interstate Highway System by more than a quarter of a century. The petition read:

> *The Association hereby requests the Secretary of Agriculture, in cooperation with the several states, to underwrite immediately the selection of and designation of a comprehensive system of through interstate routes and to devise a comprehensive and uniform scheme for designating such routes in such a manner as to give them a conspicuous place among highways of the country as roads of interstate and national significance.*

With more than fifteen million automobiles traveling the nation's vastly underdeveloped road system, Department of Agriculture officials were quick to acknowledge the soundness of the association's request. During the following year, Congress passed the Federal Aid Highway Act, which not only authorized a nationwide system of federally funded roads, but also defined the numbering system by which each highway would be known. One of the thoroughfares to emerge from the planning was Route 66, originating in Chicago's Grant Park and, on the way to its final destination in Palisades Park in Santa Monica, California, traversing three time zones, more than 2,400 miles, and eight states.

The section of I-40 replacing Route 66 around Williams honored that autumn day in 1984 had been a long time coming. The culprit in the old thoroughfare's demise was President Dwight D. Eisenhower's monumental National Highway Program, proposed to Congress on February 22, 1955. The massive $101 billion program involved government from all levels—federal, state, and local—and anticipated a system that would reduce highway fatalities, improve the quality of existing infrastructure, provide means for evacuation from target areas in case of nuclear attack, and reduce traffic congestion on the nation's highways. Eisenhower suggested that

A sound Federal highway program, I believe, can
and should stand on its own feet, with highway users
providing the total dollars necessary for improvement
and new construction. Financing of interstate and
Federal-aid systems should be based on the planned use
of increasing revenues from present gas and diesel oil
taxes, augmented in limited instances with tolls.

Sixteen months later, Congress authorized an expenditure of thirty-three billion dollars for Eisenhower's highway program.

Over the next few years, four-lane interstate highways were constructed all over the United States, from the Atlantic Ocean to the Pacific and from the Gulf of Mexico to the Canadian border, with enhancements and modifications continuing to this day. One of these monster thoroughfares, and the road that sent Route 66 to its grave, was Interstate 40, which runs from just outside Wilmington, North Carolina, to Barstow, California. Entering Arizona from the east near Lupton, the road traverses the entire east-west width of the state, exiting by crossing the Colorado River into California near Topock.

Historic Route 66 ran close to or through several fascinating natural and cultural sites in the state of Arizona: part of the Painted Desert, the Petrified Forest, the Meteor Crater, Walnut Canyon, Bill Williams Mountain, the Hualapai Indian Reservation, among others, as well as many typical American towns and communities, such as Lupton, Holbrook, Winslow, Winona, Flagstaff, Williams, Seligman, Kingman, Yucca, and Topock. Within a few years of its construction, Route 66 attained legendary status as the "Main Street of America," a reputation no doubt enhanced by books such as John Steinbeck's *The Grapes of Wrath,* in which the author introduced America to destitute refugees fleeing the great Dust Bowl of the 1930s and heading to the rainbow's end in California. Steinbeck wrote, "And they come into 66 from the tributary side roads, from the wagon tracks and the rutted country roads, 66 is the mother road, the road of flight." Then, in 1946, Bobby Troup, a songwriter and former member of Tommy Dorsey's band, penned a song that would further immortalize the road. "Get Your Kicks on Route 66" was recorded by the great Nat "King" Cole and became an overnight sensation.

Today, one can still see the natural beauties of the region through which the legendary Route 66 once passed while driving across the state along I-40. But to really enjoy the wonders and the down-to-earth pleasures of the towns and the people along the way—the tourist courts and motels, cafes, Indian markets, trading posts, pie wagons, filling stations, and souvenir shops—one must leave the freeway and visit what is left of those sights, sounds, and smells that once thrilled generations of American travelers along the "Mother Road" of America.

THE RODEO-CHEDISKI FIRE

2002

On June 25, 2002, President George W. Bush stood before a handful of evacuees in the small town of Eagar, about eighteen miles from the New Mexico border near the entrance of Arizona's Apache-Sitgreaves National Forest. His audience was part of the estimated thirty thousand people who had fled their homes in the wake of a series of vicious wildfires that had swept the region over the prior few days. The president had stopped at Eagar on his way to a G8 Summit meeting in Canada to witness for himself the tremendous devastation that had visited the area and to announce that a state of "major disaster" had been declared to provide residents with federal assistance in the form of emergency housing and relief funds. As he scanned the faces of the tired, hungry, sleepless refugees, President Bush declared, "This is a tough moment. . . . One house lost is too many houses lost, but there have been thousands of houses saved, too, and that's important."

President Bush was referring to the damage caused to a vast area of eastern Arizona, particularly the nearby national forest and the Fort Apache Indian Reservation, by what became known as the Rodeo-Chediski Fire. As Bush spoke, this gigantic conflagration—actually the results of the merger of two separate and at one time distant blazes—had burned more than 360,000 acres of ponderosa pine, brush, chaparral, and juniper, destroying 345 homes in its wake. Before it was through, its hungry flames would consume close to 470,000 acres, giving it the dubious honor of being Arizona's largest and most destructive forest fire in history.

Although June usually marks the beginning of Arizona's so-called "monsoon" season, when rainfall becomes more plentiful, the year 2002 was not living up to expectations. Already the region had been victim to a several-year-long, persistent drought that had made most of its forests and grasslands tinder dry. Snowfall in previous years had diminished as well, leaving the water table far below normal and fire conditions growing stronger with each succeeding day. Mother Nature might have averted the horrific fire had she been the only player in the vast drama that was about to unfold. But the human factor also had its role, and it was a man in one case and a woman in the other who set the forests ablaze.

The Fort Apache Indian Reservation sprawls over nearly 1.7 million acres of Apache, Gila, and Navajo Counties and is home to around twelve thousand members of the White Mountain Apache tribe. Situated just south of the Mogollon Rim, it shares a common boundary with the San Carlos Apache Indian Reservation to the south. Lying off U.S. Highway 60, between the towns of Globe and Show Low, is the village of Cibecue. Following the road leading to Cibecue from U.S. 60, one crosses the Cibecue Pass, providing a magnificent view encompassing thousands of acres of the reservation as well as the neighboring Apache-Sitgreaves National Forest.

Close to Cibecue sits an antiquated rodeo grounds, used from time to time by the Apaches for horse-oriented events such as bull riding and bronco busting. On June 18, 2002, a young Apache man, who once had been a contract firefighter on the reservation, wandered the dilapidated arena, contemplating the past. For reasons still unknown, he reached in his pocket, retrieved a match, ignited it, and dropped the flame to the ground amid the dry grass. Within minutes, the hungry flames had consumed several square yards. Continuing to grow, they soon lashed out at the scrub brush and forest nearby. Ugly black smoke belched to the sky as the fire attacked every piece of flammable material in its path. By this point the young man had become frightened and made his exit, but the conflagration was quickly spreading across close to three hundred acres of reservation land.

Within two days, the Rodeo fire, as the blaze would now be called, had gobbled up nearly thirty thousand acres. In the meantime, another fire, inadvertently set in motion by a stranded female hiker as she lit a fire to signal a rescue helicopter, was spreading out of control near Chediski Peak and the communities of Heber and Overgaard—about twenty-seven miles north, as the crow flies, from the Rodeo blaze. By Sunday afternoon, the two fires were less than one mile apart and had sent close to twenty-five thousand terrified residents of the Mogollon Rim scurrying for safety. It was just a matter of time before the two blazes would combine.

Over the next two weeks, the united Rodeo-Chediski fire destroyed an area equivalent to a piece of real estate measuring twenty-seven miles on each side. About 60 percent of the burned area was on the Indian reservation, while approximately 38 percent was on destroyed national forestlands. The price tag for the tragedy was $153 million dollars. More than four hundred structures were destroyed, and over thirty thousand residents of the vast region were displaced.

Tragic wildfires have struck Arizona both before and after the great Rodeo-Chediski blaze. In June 1990, six firefighters were killed near Payson as they fought flames that eventually destroyed twenty-eight thousand acres of forest and sixty-three buildings, including Zane Grey's cabin. The state's second largest fire in history occurred north of Phoenix Valley in June 2005, when nearly one-quarter of a million acres was destroyed. Both of these blazes were caused by lightning.

Despite the best efforts of both Forest Service officials and environmentalists, forest fires will, unfortunately, continue to occur in Arizona so long as precipitation is scarce, the temperatures reach record highs, and the landscape remains parched.

ARIZONA FACTS
AND TRIVIA

- Arizona is the sixth largest state in the nation after Alaska, Texas, California, Montana, and New Mexico. It encompasses 114,000 square miles, or almost 73 million acres. It averages 340 miles from east to west, and the maximum distance from north to south is 395 miles.

- The mean elevation of Arizona is 4,100 feet. The highest point is Humphreys Peak in Coconino County, at 12,633 feet. The lowest point is on the Colorado River at Yuma, at seventy feet.

- The geographical center of Arizona is fifty-five miles southeast of Prescott in Yavapai County.

- In 2000, Arizona had a population of 5,130,632. Its estimated population in 2008 was 6,500,180.

- The state ranks sixteenth in the nation for population.

- The coldest temperature ever recorded in Arizona was minus forty degrees Fahrenheit on January 7, 1971, at Hawley Lake. The average low temperature in Phoenix in January is thirty-nine degrees.

- The hottest temperature was 128 degrees on June 29, 1994, at Lake Havasu City. The average high temperature in Phoenix in July is 105 degrees.

- Arizona became a U.S. Territory in 1863. It became the forty-eighth state on February 14, 1912.

- Phoenix is both the capital of Arizona and its largest city, with a population in 2000 of 1,321,045. Its estimated population in 2006 was 1,512,986.

- Arizona contains fifteen counties: Mohave, Coconino, Yavapai, Navajo, Apache, La Paz, Maricopa, Gila, Greenlee, Yuma, Pinal, Graham, Pima, Cochise, and Santa Cruz.

- The word *Arizona* is derived from an Indian word meaning "place of small springs."

- The state motto is *Ditat Deus,* or "God Enriches."

- Arizona's official state nickname is "The Grand Canyon State."

- The state bird is the cactus wren (*Campylorhynchus brunneicapillus*).

- The state flower is the saguaro cactus blossom (*Carnegiea gigantea*), and the state tree is the paloverde. There are two species of paloverde, the blue (*Cercidium floridum*) and the yellow (*Cercidium microphyllum*).

- The state gemstone is turquoise.

- The state fossil is petrified wood.

- The state song is "Arizona March Song," with lyrics by Margaret Rowe Clifford and music by Maurice Blumenthal, adopted in 1919. The song "Arizona," by Rex Allen, Jr., was adopted as an alternative in 1982.

- The state flag consists of a copper-colored, five-pointed star—symbolic of the state's copper wealth—in the center of a field that is blue on the bottom half. On the top half, six yellow and seven red rays radiate from the star.

- Some famous Arizonans include Apache chiefs Cochise and Geronimo, Supreme Court Justice Sandra Day O'Connor, statesman Barry Goldwater, singer Linda Ronstadt, humorist Erma Bombeck, and 2008 Republican presidential nominee John McCain.

BIBLIOGRAPHY

Adams, Alexander B. *Geronimo*. New York: G.P. Putnam's Sons, 1971.

Apache Chronicle. New York: The World Publishing Company, 1972.

Arizona Highways, Vol. 60, No. 4. Phoenix: Arizona Department of Transportation, 1984.

Bartlett, John Russell. *Personal Narrative of Explorations and Incidents in Texas, New Mexico, California, Sonora, and Chihuahua*. Volume Two. New York: D. Appleton & Company, 1854.

Batman, Richard. *American Ecclesiastes*. New York: Harcourt Brace Jovanovich, Publishers, 1984.

Bolton, Herbert Eugene. *The Padre on Horseback*. Chicago: Loyola University Press, 1986.

Clayton, Wallace E. *The* Tombstone Epitaph *and John Philip Clum*. Tombstone, Ariz.: Red Marie's, 1985.

Commager, Henry Steele, ed. *Documents of American History*. New York: Appleton-Century-Crofts, Inc., 1958.

Condition of the Indian Tribes. Report of the Joint Special Committee, Appointed Under Joint Resolution of March 3, 1865, with an Appendix. Washington, D.C.: Senate Document No. 156. 39th Congress, 2nd Session, 1867.

Conkling, Roscoe P., and Margaret B. Conkling. *The Butterfield Overland Mail 1857–1869*. Glendale, Calif.: The Arthur H. Clark Company, 1947.

Cooke, Philip St. George. *The Conquest of New Mexico and California in 1846–1847*. Chicago: The Rio Grande Press, 1964.

———. "Report of Lieut. Col. P. St. George Cooke of His March from Santa Fe, New Mexico to San Diego, Upper California," in Emory, Lieut. Col. W. H. *Notes of a Military Reconnoissance, from Fort Leavenworth, in Missouri, to San Diego, in California, etc.* Washington, D.C.: Executive Document No. 41, 30th Congress, 1st Session, 1848.

Couper, Heather, and Nigel Henbest. *New Worlds: In Search of the Planets*. Reading, Mass.: Addison-Wesley Publishing Company, 1986.

Cremony, John C. *Life Among the Apaches*. San Francisco: A. Roman & Company, 1868. Reprinted New York: Indian Head Books, 1991.

Dary, David. *Entrepreneurs of the Old West*. New York: Alfred A. Knopf, 1986.

Day, A. Grove. *Coronado's Quest*. Berkeley: University of California Press, 1964.

Dictionary of American Biography. Supplement 7. New York: Charles Scribner's Sons, 1981.

Emory, Lieut. Col. W.H. *Notes of a Military Reconnoissance, from Fort Leavenworth, in Missouri, to San Diego, in California, etc.* Washington, D.C.: Executive Document No. 41, 30th Congress, 1st Session, 1848.

Encyclopedia of Science and Technology. 7th Edition. Volume 5. New York: McGraw-Hill, Inc., 1992.

Fagan, Brian M. *The Adventure of Archaeology*. Washington, D.C.: National Geographic Society, 1985.

The Far Planets. Alexandria, Va.: Time-Life Books, 1988.

Faulk, Odie B. *Destiny Road: The Gila Trail and the Opening of the Southwest*. New York: Oxford University Press, 1973.

Faust, Patricia L., ed. *Historical Times Illustrated Encyclopedia of the Civil War*. New York: Harper & Row, Publishers, 1986.

Forrest, Earle R. *Missions and Pueblos of the Old Southwest*. Chicago: The Rio Grande Press, 1965.

Fowler, Arlen L. *The Black Infantry in the West 1869–1891*. Westport, N.Y.: Greenwood Publishing Corp., 1971.

Garrett, Pat. *The Authentic Life of Billy, the Kid*. Norman: University of Oklahoma Press, 1954.

Goetzmann, William H. *Army Exploration in the American West, 1803–1863*. Lincoln: University of Nebraska Press, 1979.

Goldwater, Barry M., with Jack Casserly. *Goldwater*. New York: Doubleday, 1988.

Guttman, Jon. "Unpleasant Valley War." *Wild West* magazine. Leesburg, Va.: Empire Press, October, 1990.

Harris, Benjamin Butler. *The Gila Trail: The Texas Argonauts and the California Gold Rush*. Norman: University of Oklahoma Press, 1960.

Herr, Pamela. *Jessie Benton Fremont*. New York: Franklin Watts, 1987.

Holdcroft, Gary Phillip. *Walking Through the Ashes: A Volunteer Firefighter's Perspective of the Rodeo-Chediski Fire*. Vancouver BC: Trafford Publishing Company, 2004.

Jackson, Carlton. *Zane Grey*. Boston: Twayne Publishers, 1973.

Johnston, Capt. A.R. "Journal of Captain A.R. Johnston, First Dragoons." *See* Emory 1848.

Lamar, Howard R., ed. *The Reader's Encyclopedia of the American West*. New York: Harper & Row, Publishers, 1986.

Leckie, William H. *The Buffalo Soldiers: A Narrative of the Negro Cavalry in the West*. Norman: University of Oklahoma Press, 1967.

"Letter from the Secretary of War." Washington, D.C.: Senate Executive Document No. 117, 49th Congress, 2nd Session, 1887.

Levernier, James, and Cohen Hennig, eds. *The Indians and Their Captives*. Westport, Conn.: Greenwood Press, 1977.

Lister, Robert H., and Florence C. Lister. *Those Who Came Before*. Globe, Ariz.: Southwest Parks and Monuments Association, 1983.

Manchester, Ann and Albert. "The Hubbell Trading Post: Historic Gem of the Southwest." *Persimmon Hill* magazine. Oklahoma City: The National Cowboy Hall of Fame, Summer, 1992.

McNitt, Frank. *The Indian Traders*. Norman: University of Oklahoma Press, 1989.

Metz, Leon C. *The Shooters*. El Paso: Mangan Books, 1986.

Moorhead, Max L. *The Presidio: Bastion of the Spanish Borderlands*. Norman: University of Oklahoma Press, 1975.

Nash, Jay Robert. *Encyclopedia of Western Lawmen & Outlaws*. New York: Paragon House, 1992.

Nolan, Frederick. *The Lincoln County War: A Documentary History*. Norman: University of Oklahoma Press, 1992.

Pattie, James Ohio. *The Personal Narrative of James O. Pattie*. Philadelphia: J.B. Lippincott Company, 1962.

Peckham, Howard H. *Captured by Indians*. New Brunswick, N.J.: Rutgers University Press, 1954.

Powell, J. W. *Canyons of the Colorado*. New York: Flood & Vincent, 1895. Reprinted as *The Exploration of the Colorado River and Its Canyons*. New York: Dover Publications, Inc., 1961.

Procter, Gil. *The Trails of Pete Kitchen*. Tucson, Ariz.: Dale Stuart King, 1964.

Report of the Secretary of War. Washington, D.C.: Executive Document No. 43. 35th Congress, 1st Session, 1858.

Sides, Hampton. *Blood and Thunder: An Epic of the American West*. New York: Doubleday, 2006.

Sifakis, Carl. *Encyclopedia of American Crime*. New York: Fact on File, Inc., 1982.

Sitgreaves, Lorenzo. *Report of an Expedition Down the Zuni and Colorado Rivers*. Washington, D.C.: Executive Document No. 59, 32nd Congress, 2nd Session, 1853.

Stratton, Royal B. *Life Among the Indians: Being an Interesting Narrative of the Captivity of the Oatman Girls*. San Francisco: Whitton, Towne & Co's Excelsior Steam Power Presses, 1857. Reprinted several times as *Captivity of the Oatman Girls*.

Terrell, John Upton. *American Indian Almanac*. New York: The World Publishing Company, 1971.

Thrapp, Dan L. *Encyclopedia of Frontier Biography*. Glendale, Calif.: The Arthur H. Clark Company, 1988.

Time magazine. Feb. 10, 1930; March 24, 1930; Oct. 7, 1935; March 9, 1936.

The Tombstone Epitaph. Volume I, Number 1. Tombstone, Ariz., May 1, 1880. Reprinted in 1980 by The Tombstone Epitaph.

Wagoner, Jay J. *Arizona Territory, 1863–1912: A Political History.* Tucson: University of Arizona Press, 1970.

Walker, Dale L. *Death Was the Black Horse.* Austin, Tex.: Madrona Press, Inc., 1975.

Wallis, Michael. *Route 66: The Mother Road.* New York: St. Martin's Griffin, 2001.

Wellman, Paul I. *The Indian Wars of the West.* New York: Modern Literary Editions Publishing Company, n.d.

Wilbur, Ray Lyman, and Northcutt Ely. *The Hoover Dam Documents.* Washington, D.C.: U.S. Government Printing Office, House Document No. 717, 80th Congress, 2nd Session, 1948.

General Sources

http://cnn.news (CNN News)

http://news.bbc.co.uk (British Broadcasting Company)

www.wilderness.com (The Wilderness Society)

INDEX

ABOUT THE AUTHOR

James A. Crutchfield is a western historian who has written numerous books, including *It Happened in Texas, It Happened in Washington,* and seven other It Happened In titles; forty books about American history; and hundreds of articles for newspapers, journals, and national magazines, among them *The Magazine Antiques, Early American Life,* and *The American Cowboy.* He has won writing awards from Western Writers of America, the American Association for State and Local History, and the Tennessee Revolutionary Bicentennial Commission. A former board member of the Tennessee Historical Society, he sits on the Board of National Scholars for President's Park in Williamsburg, Virginia. He and his wife, Regena, reside in a pre–Civil War home in Tennessee.